Symfony2 Essentials

A fast-paced developer's guide to using Symfony2
to make your everyday web development work
more efficient

Wojciech Bancer

open source*
community experience distilled

[PACKT]
PUBLISHING
BIRMINGHAM - MUMBAI

Symfony2 Essentials

Copyright © 2015 Packt Publishing

All rights reserved. No part of this book may be reproduced, stored in a retrieval system, or transmitted in any form or by any means, without the prior written permission of the publisher, except in the case of brief quotations embedded in critical articles or reviews.

Every effort has been made in the preparation of this book to ensure the accuracy of the information presented. However, the information contained in this book is sold without warranty, either express or implied. Neither the author, nor Packt Publishing, and its dealers and distributors will be held liable for any damages caused or alleged to be caused directly or indirectly by this book.

Packt Publishing has endeavored to provide trademark information about all of the companies and products mentioned in this book by the appropriate use of capitals. However, Packt Publishing cannot guarantee the accuracy of this information.

First published: September 2015

Production reference: 1040915

Published by Packt Publishing Ltd.
Livery Place
35 Livery Street
Birmingham B3 2PB, UK.

ISBN 978-1-78439-876-7

www.packtpub.com

Credits

Author

Wojciech Bancer

Reviewers

Cristian Bujoreanu

Olivier Pons

Commissioning Editor

Usha Iyer

Acquisition Editor

Reshma Raman

Content Development Editor

Arwa Manasawala

Technical Editor

Shiny Poojary

Copy Editor

Kausambhi Majumdar

Project Coordinator

Shweta H Birwatkar

Proofreader

Safis Editing

Indexer

Tejal Soni

Production Coordinator

Manu Joseph

Cover Work

Manu Joseph

About the Author

Wojciech Bancer has a master's degree in computer science. He has over 10 years of experience in web application development. In 2007, after passing the Zend exam, he received a Zend Certified Engineer for PHP5 certificate. He started his career as a freelancer and consultant by developing web applications in PHP 4 and PHP 5. He has led many IT projects for clients in Europe and USA. Currently, Wojciech is a managing partner of a software organization and is in charge of the R&D structure of one of the fastest growing iBeacon projects in Europe.

About the Reviewers

Cristian Bujoreanu is a web developer originally from Romania and is currently based in Zürich, Switzerland. He specializes in web development and has a solid understanding of web application development processes, right from layout / user interface to relational database structures. He creates usable, professional, and user-friendly web applications according to the latest standards and innovative technologies.

Cristian has been in this field for nearly 7 years. He loves his work and enjoys every new project that he's involved in. After spending 4 years working for two web agencies in Romania, he moved to Switzerland in early 2012. He joined joiz, a social TV station with headquarters in Zürich. In February 2015, he started a new venture at Teamup Solutions AG.

Olivier Pons is a senior developer who has been building websites since 1997. He's a teacher at the University of Sciences (IUT) in Aix-en-Provence in France, ISEN (Institut Supérieur de l'Électronique et du Numérique), G4 Marseille, and École d'Ingénieurs des Mines de Gardanne. He teaches state-of-the-art web techniques in NodeJS, big data / NoSQL, the fundamentals of MVC, the basics of Symfony, WordPress, PHP, HTML, CSS, jQuery and jQuery Mobile, AngularJS, Apache, the basics of Linux, and advanced VIM techniques. He has already done some technical reviews, including the Packt Publishing books *Learning ExtJS*, *Ext JS 4 First Look*, *jQuery hotshot*, *jQuery Mobile Web Development Essentials*, *Wordpress 4.x Complete*, and *jQuery 2.0 for Designers Beginner's Guide*, among others. In 2011, Olivier left a full-time job as a Delphi developer and PHP expert to concentrate on his own company, HQF Development (`http://hqf.fr`). He runs a number of websites, including `http://krystallopolis.fr`, `http://artsgaleries.com`, `http://www.battlesoop.fr`, `http://www.livrepizzas.fr`, `http://www.papdevis.fr`, and `http://olivierpons.fr`, his own web development blog. Currently, he's learning Unity and building a game on his own. He works as a consultant, teacher, and project manager. Sometimes, he also helps big companies as a senior and highly skilled developer.

www.PacktPub.com

Support files, eBooks, discount offers, and more

For support files and downloads related to your book, please visit www.PacktPub.com.

Did you know that Packt offers eBook versions of every book published, with PDF and ePub files available? You can upgrade to the eBook version at www.PacktPub.com and as a print book customer, you are entitled to a discount on the eBook copy. Get in touch with us at service@packtpub.com for more details.

At www.PacktPub.com, you can also read a collection of free technical articles, sign up for a range of free newsletters and receive exclusive discounts and offers on Packt books and eBooks.

https://www2.packtpub.com/books/subscription/packtlib

Do you need instant solutions to your IT questions? PacktLib is Packt's online digital book library. Here, you can search, access, and read Packt's entire library of books.

Why subscribe?

- Fully searchable across every book published by Packt
- Copy and paste, print, and bookmark content
- On demand and accessible via a web browser

Free access for Packt account holders

If you have an account with Packt at www.PacktPub.com, you can use this to access PacktLib today and view 9 entirely free books. Simply use your login credentials for immediate access.

Table of Contents

Preface

PHP is currently one of the most popular languages in web development. Over time, the language itself has grown and become more mature. However, it still lacks good design patterns and good habits "by design". You can write a very good code with it, but you can also write very bad "spaghetti code".

Symfony2 is currently one of the most popular frameworks to speed up PHP development. It greatly helps you to create clean and reusable code, and it is the first framework that takes modern design patterns like DependencyInjection very seriously. It is also the first framework that uses features of PHP 5.3—namespaces, closures, and so on. By using this framework, you will be able to deliver more advanced and complicated web applications, suitable even for enterprise requirements.

What this book covers

Chapter 1, The Symfony Framework – Installation and Configuration, gives a quick overview of Symfony's history, ways to install and configure it, and ways to use the composer—the dependency manager used within Symfony2.

Chapter 2, Your First Pages, gives you a quick walkthrough over the basic MVC features available in most solutions nowadays. It will demonstrate to you how to create simple controllers and first views, prepare entities, and load sample data.

Chapter 3, Twig Templating and Assets Handling, shows you in details how to handle views, assets managements, and add a frontend library.

Chapter 4, Forms, focuses on form creation. It will show you how to create form types, validate forms, and write data to databases.

Chapter 5, Security and Handling Users, gives you information about Symfony security features. In this chapter, we will create an example of registration and login forms, and how to handle users with the help of an open source bundle.

Chapter 6, Translation, gives information about translation and internalization. You will learn how to create translation files, translate various areas of your application, and choose a good translation strategy.

Chapter 7, AJAX, teaches you how to handle basic AJAX calls. We will also learn about bundles that are useful when you write RESTful applications, how to handle various HTTP methods, and how to serialize data in a JSON structure.

Chapter 8, Command-line Operations, will provide you with examples on how to create a command-line task, which is often useful with tasks executed in background (cron tasks). You will also learn how to send an e-mail through swiftmailer—a component used by default within the Symfony framework to handle e-mail sending.

Chapter 9, Symfony2 Profiler and Debugger, is where you will learn about the Web Debug Toolbar and profiler. We will examine the possibilities offered by these tools and write some code to demonstrate debugging and profiling features.

Chapter 10, Preparing an Application for Production, will give you an overview of the tasks that are usually done when your project needs to be deployed. You will also get an overview of various deployment strategies, and you will be able to check your framework and bundles against known security issues.

What you need for this book

You will need a minimum of a PHP 5.4 installation with standard extensions such as database, intl, mcrypt, posix, or pcntl. It is also recommended for this book to use a Unix/Linux system such as Debian, Ubuntu, Red Hat, FreeBSD, or Mac OS X.

Who this book is for

This book is aimed at experienced programmers, especially those familiar with a closely related technology such as Yii or Laravel but who now want to learn Symfony quickly.

This book will also prove beneficial for experienced PHP developers who want to explore and evaluate new frameworks and their possibilities in day-to-day tasks.

Conventions

In this book, you will find a number of text styles that distinguish between different kinds of information. Here are some examples of these styles and an explanation of their meaning.

Code words in text, database table names, folder names, filenames, file extensions, pathnames, dummy URLs, user input, and Twitter handles are shown as follows: "Your own bundles are usually stored within the src/ directory, while the third-party bundles sit within the vendor/ directory."

A block of code is set as follows:

```
public function indexAction()
    {
        return $this->render('default/index.html.twig');
    }
```

When we wish to draw your attention to a particular part of a code block, the relevant lines or items are set in bold:

```
use AppBundle\Entity\Task;
use Symfony\Bundle\FrameworkBundle\Controller\Controller;
use Symfony\Component\HttpFoundation\Request;
```

Any command-line input or output is written as follows:

```
$ curl -sS https://getcomposer.org/installer | php
$ sudo mv composer.phar /usr/local/bin/composer
```

New terms and **important words** are shown in bold. Words that you see on the screen, for example, in menus or dialog boxes, appear in the text like this: "You should see a **Hello anonymous!** welcome text."

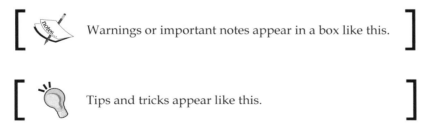

Warnings or important notes appear in a box like this.

Tips and tricks appear like this.

Reader feedback

Feedback from our readers is always welcome. Let us know what you think about this book—what you liked or disliked. Reader feedback is important for us as it helps us develop titles that you will really get the most out of.

To send us general feedback, simply e-mail feedback@packtpub.com, and mention the book's title in the subject of your message.

If there is a topic that you have expertise in and you are interested in either writing or contributing to a book, see our author guide at www.packtpub.com/authors.

Customer support

Now that you are the proud owner of a Packt book, we have a number of things to help you to get the most from your purchase.

Downloading the example code

You can download the example code files from your account at http://www.packtpub.com for all the Packt Publishing books you have purchased. If you purchased this book elsewhere, you can visit http://www.packtpub.com/support and register to have the files e-mailed directly to you.

Errata

Although we have taken every care to ensure the accuracy of our content, mistakes do happen. If you find a mistake in one of our books—maybe a mistake in the text or the code—we would be grateful if you could report this to us. By doing so, you can save other readers from frustration and help us improve subsequent versions of this book. If you find any errata, please report them by visiting http://www.packtpub.com/submit-errata, selecting your book, clicking on the **Errata Submission Form** link, and entering the details of your errata. Once your errata are verified, your submission will be accepted and the errata will be uploaded to our website or added to any list of existing errata under the Errata section of that title.

To view the previously submitted errata, go to https://www.packtpub.com/books/content/support and enter the name of the book in the search field. The required information will appear under the **Errata** section.

Piracy

Piracy of copyrighted material on the Internet is an ongoing problem across all media. At Packt, we take the protection of our copyright and licenses very seriously. If you come across any illegal copies of our works in any form on the Internet, please provide us with the location address or website name immediately so that we can pursue a remedy.

Please contact us at copyright@packtpub.com with a link to the suspected pirated material.

We appreciate your help in protecting our authors and our ability to bring you valuable content.

Questions

If you have a problem with any aspect of this book, you can contact us at questions@packtpub.com, and we will do our best to address the problem.

1
The Symfony Framework – Installation and Configuration

The Symfony framework is currently one of the most popular PHP frameworks existing within the PHP developer's environment. Version 2, which was released a few years ago, has been a great improvement, and in my opinion was one of the key elements for making the PHP ecosystem suitable for larger enterprise projects. The framework version 2.0 not only required the modern PHP version (minimal version required for Symfony is PHP 5.3.8), but also uses state-of-the-art technology — namespaces and anonymous functions. Authors also put a lot of efforts to provide long term support and to minimize changes, which break the compatibility between versions. Also, Symfony forced developers to use a few useful design concepts. The key one, introduced in Symfony, was `DependencyInjection`.

 In most cases, the book will refer to the framework as Symfony2. If you want to look over the Internet or Google about this framework, apart from using `Symfony` keyword you may also try to use the `Symfony2` keyword This was the way recommended some time ago by one of the creators to make searching or referencing to the specific framework version easier in future.

Key reasons to choose Symfony2

Symfony2 is recognized in the PHP ecosystem as a very well-written and well-maintained framework. Design patterns that are recommended and forced within the framework allow work to be more efficient in the group, this allows better tests and the creation of reusable code.

Symfony's knowledge can also be verified through a certificate system, and this allows its developers to be easily found and be more recognized on the market. Last but not least, the Symfony2 components are used as parts of other projects, for example, look at the following:

- Drupal
- phpBB
- Laravel
- eZ Publish and more

Over time, there is a good chance that you will find the parts of the Symfony2 components within other open source solutions.

Bundles and extendable architecture are also some of the key Symfony2 features.

They not only allow you to make your work easier through the easy development of reusable code, but also allows you to find smaller or larger pieces of code that you can embed and use within your project to speed up and make your work faster.

The standards of Symfony2 also make it easier to catch errors and to write high-quality code; its community is growing every year.

The history of Symfony

There are many Symfony versions around, and it's good to know the differences between them to learn how the framework was evolving during these years. The first stable Symfony version — 1.0 — was released in the beginning of 2007 and was supported for three years. In mid-2008, version 1.1 was presented, which wasn't compatible with the previous release, and it was difficult to upgrade any old project to this.

Symfony 1.2 version was released shortly after this, at the end of 2008. Migrating between these versions was much easier, and there were no dramatic changes in the structure. The final versions of Symfony 1's legacy family was released nearly one year later. Simultaneously, there were two version releases, 1.3 and 1.4. Both were identical, but Symfony 1.4 did not have deprecated features, and it was recommended to start new projects with it. Version 1.4 had 3 years of support.

If you look into the code, version 1.x was very different from version 2. The company that was behind Symfony (the French company, SensioLabs) made a bold move and decided to rewrite the whole framework from scratch.

The first release of Symfony2 wasn't perfect, but it was very promising. It relied on Git submodules (the composer did not exist back then). The 2.1 and 2.2 versions were closer to the one we use now, although it required a lot of effort to migrate to the upper level. Finally, the Symfony 2.3 was released — the first long-term support version within the 2.x branch. After this version, the changes provided within the next major versions (2.4, 2.5, and 2.6) are not so drastic and usually they do not break compatibility.

> This book was written based on the latest stable Symfony 2.7.4 version and was tested with PHP 5.5). This Symfony version is marked as the so called long-term support version, and updates for it will be released for 3 years since the first 2.7 version release.

Installation

Prior to installing Symfony2, you don't need to have a configured web server. If you have at least PHP version 5.4, you can use the standalone server provided by Symfony2. This server is suitable for development purposes and should not be used for production. It is strongly recommend to work with a Linux/UNIX system for both development and production deployment of Symfony2 framework applications. While it is possible to install and operate on a Windows box, due to its different nature, working with Windows can sometimes force you to maintain a separate fragment of code for this system.

> Even if your primary OS is Windows, it is strongly recommended to configure Linux system in a virtual environment. Also, there are solutions that will help you in automating the whole process. As an example, see more on `https://www.vagrantup.com/` website.

To install Symfony2, you can use a few methods as follows:

- Use a new Symfony2 installer script (currently, the only officially recommended). Please note that installer requires at least PHP 5.4.
- Use a composer dependency manager to install a Symfony project.
- Download a `zip` or `tgz` package and unpack it.
- It does not really matter which method you choose, as they all give you similar results.

Installing Symfony2 using an installer

To install Symfony2 through an installer, go to the Symfony website at `http://symfony.com/download`, and install the Symfony2 installer by issuing the following commands:

```
$ sudo curl -LsS http://symfony.com/installer -o /usr/local/bin/symfony
$ sudo chmod +x /usr/local/bin/symfony
```

After this, you can install Symfony by just typing the following command:

```
$ symfony new <new_project_folder>
```

To install the Symfony2 framework for a to-do application, execute the following command:

```
$ symfony new todoapp
```

This command installs the latest Symfony2 stable version on the newly created `todoapp` folder, creates the Symfony2 application, and prepares some basic structure for you to work with.

After the app creation, you can verify that your local PHP is properly configured for Symfony2 by typing the following command:

```
$ php app/check.php
```

If everything goes fine, the script should complete with the following message:

```
[OK]
Your system is ready to run Symfony projects
```

Symfony2 is equipped with a standalone server. It makes development easier. If you want to run this, type the following command:

```
$ php app/console server:run
```

If everything went alright, you will see a message that your server is working on the IP 127.0.0.1 and port 8000. If there is an error, make sure you are not running anything else that is listening on port 8000. It is also possible to run the server on a different port or IP, if you have such a requirement, by adding the address and port as a parameter, that is:

```
$ php app/console server:run 127.0.0.1:8080
```

If everything works, you can now type the following:

```
http://127.0.0.1:8000/
```

Now, you will visit Symfony's welcome page.

This page presents you with a nice welcome information and useful documentation link.

Downloading the example code

You can download the example code files for all Packt books you have purchased from your account at http://www.packtpub.com. If you have purchased this book elsewhere, you can visit http://www.packtpub.com/support and register to have the files directly e-mailed to you.

The Symfony2 directory structure

Let's dive in to the initial directory structure within the typical Symfony application. Here it is:

- app
- bin
- src
- vendor
- web

While Symfony2 is very flexible in terms of directory structure, it is recommended to keep the basic structure mentioned earlier.

The following table describes their purpose:

Directory	Used for
app	This holds information about general configuration, routing, security configuration, database parameters, and many others. It is also the recommended place for putting new view files. This directory is a starting point.
bin	It holds some helper executables. It is not really important during the development process, and rarely modified.
src	This directory holds the project PHP code (usually your bundles).

Directory	Used for
vendor	These are third-party libraries used within the project. Usually, this directory contains all the open source third-party bundles, libraries, and other resources. It's worth to mention that it's recommended to keep the files within this directory outside the versioning system. It means that you should not modify them under any circumstances. Fortunately, there are ways to modify the code, if it suits your needs more. This will be demonstrated when we implement user management within our to-do application.
web	This is the directory that is accessible through the web server. It holds the main entry point to the application (usually the app.php and app_dev.php files), CSS files, JavaScript files, and all the files that need to be available through the web server (user uploadable files).

So, in most cases, you will be usually modifying and creating the PHP files within the src/ directory, the view and configuration files within the app/ directory, and the JS/CSS files within the web/ directory.

The main directory also holds a few files as follows:

* .gitignore
* README.md
* composer.json
* composer.lock

The .gitignore file's purpose is to provide some preconfigured settings for the Git repository, while the composer.json and composer.lock files are the files used by the composer dependency manager.

What is a bundle?

Within the Symfony2 application, you will be using the "bundle" term quite often. Bundle is something similar to plugins. So it can literally hold any code controllers, views, models, and services. A bundle can integrate other non-Symfony2 libraries and hold some JavaScript/CSS code as well. We can say that almost everything is a bundle in Symfony2; even some of the core framework features together form a bundle. A bundle usually implements a single feature or functionality. The code you are writing when you write a Symfony2 application is also a bundle.

There are two types of bundles. The first kind of bundle is the one you write within the application, which is project-specific and not reusable. For this purpose, there is a special bundle called AppBundle created for you when you install the Symfony2 project.

Also, there are reusable bundles that are shared across the various projects either written by you, your team, or provided by a third-party vendors. Your own bundles are usually stored within the `src/` directory, while the third-party bundles sit within the `vendor/` directory.

The vendor directory is used to store third-party libraries and is managed by the composer. As such, it should never be modified by you.

There are many reusable open source bundles, which help you to implement various features within the application. You can find many of them to help you with User Management, writing RESTful APIs, making better documentation, connecting to Facebook and AWS, and even generating a whole admin panel. There are tons of bundles, and everyday brings new ones.

 If you want to explore open source bundles, and want to look around what's available, I recommend you to start with the `http://knpbundles.com/` website.

The bundle name is correlated with the PHP namespace. As such, it needs to follow some technical rules, and it needs to end with the `Bundle` suffix. A few examples of correct names are `AppBundle` and `AcmeDemoBundle`, `CompanyBlogBundle` or `CompanySocialForumBundle`, and so on.

Composer

Symfony2 is built based on components, and it would be very difficult to manage the dependencies between them and the framework without a dependency manager. To make installing and managing these components easier, Symfony2 uses a manager called composer.

You can get it from the `https://getcomposer.org/` website. The composer makes it easy to install and check all dependencies, download them, and integrate them to your work. If you want to find additional packages that can be installed with the composer, you should visit `https://packagist.org/`. This site is the main composer repository, and contains information about most of the packages that are installable with the composer.

To install the composer, go to `https://getcomposer.org/download/` and see the download instruction. The download instruction should be similar to the following:

```
$ curl -sS https://getcomposer.org/installer | php
```

If the download was successful, you should see the `composer.phar` file in your directory. Move this to the project location in the same place where you have the `composer.json` and `composer.lock` files. You can also install it globally, if you prefer to, with these two commands:

```
$ curl -sS https://getcomposer.org/installer | php
$ sudo mv composer.phar /usr/local/bin/composer
```

You will usually need to use only three composer commands: `require`, `install`, and `update`.

The `require` command is executed when you need to add a new dependency. The `install` command is used to install the package. The `update` command is used when you need to fetch the latest version of your dependencies as specified within the JSON file.

The difference between install and update is subtle, but very important. If you are executing the `update` command, your `composer.lock` file gets updated with the version of the code you just fetched and downloaded. The `install` command uses the information stored in the `composer.lock` file and the fetch version stored in this file.

When to use install? For example, if you deploy the code to the server, you should use `install` rather than `update`, as it will deploy the version of the code stored in `composer.lock`, rather than download the latest version (which may be untested by you). Also, if you work in a team and you just got an update through Git, you should use `install` to fetch the vendor code updated by other developers.

You should use the `update` command if you want to check whether there is an updated version of the package you have installed, that is, whether a new minor version of Symfony2 will be released, then the `update` command will fetch everything.

As an example, let's install one extra package for user management called `FOSUserBundle` (**FOS** is a shortcut of **Friends of Symfony**). We will only install it here; we will not configure it. We will configure it in the chapter focused on security and user management.

To install `FOSUserBundle`, we need to know the correct package name and version. The easiest way is to look in the packagist site at `https://packagist.org/` and search for the package there. If you type `fosuserbundle`, the search should return a package called `friendsofsymfony/user-bundle` as one of the top results. The download counts visible on the right-hand side might be also helpful in determining how popular the bundle is.

If you click on this, you will end up on the page with the detailed information about that bundle, such as homepage, versions, and requirements of the package.

Type the following command:

```
$ php composer.phar require friendsofsymfony/user-bundle ^1.3
Using version ^1.3 for friendsofsymfony/user-bundle
./composer.json has been updated
Loading composer repositories with package information
Updating dependencies (including require-dev)
  - Installing friendsofsymfony/user-bundle (v1.3.6)
    Loading from cache


friendsofsymfony/user-bundle suggests installing willdurand/propel-
typehintable-behavior (Needed when using the propel implementation)
Writing lock file
Generating autoload files
      ...
```

Which version of the package you choose is up to you. If you are interested in package versioning standards, see the composer website at `https://getcomposer.org/doc/01-basic-usage.md#package-versions` to get more information on it.

The composer holds all the configurable information about dependencies and where to install them in a special JSON file called `composer.json`. Let's take a look at this:

```
{
"name": "wbancer/todoapp",
"license": "proprietary",
"type": "project",
"autoload": {
  "psr-0": {
    "": "src/",
    "SymfonyStandard": "app/SymfonyStandard/"
  }
},
"require": {
  "php": ">=5.3.9",
  "symfony/symfony": "2.7.*",
  "doctrine/orm": "~2.2,>=2.2.3,<2.5",
  // [...]
  "incenteev/composer-parameter-handler": "~2.0",
  "friendsofsymfony/user-bundle": "^1.3"
},
"require-dev": {
  "sensio/generator-bundle": "~2.3"
},
```

```
"scripts": {
  "post-root-package-install": [
  "SymfonyStandard\\Composer::hookRootPackageInstall"
  ],
  "post-install-cmd": [
  // post installation steps
  ],
  "post-update-cmd": [
  // post update steps
  ]
},
"config": {
  "bin-dir": "bin"
},
"extra": {
  // [...]
}
}
```

The most important section is the one with the `require` key. It holds all the information about the packages we want to use within the project. The key scripts contain a set of instructions to run post-install and post-update. The `extra` key in this case contains some settings specific to the Symfony2 framework. Note that one of the values in here points out to the `parameter.yml` file. This file is the main file holding the custom machine-specific parameters. The meaning of the other keys is rather obvious.

If you look into the `vendor/` directory, you will notice that our package has been installed in the `vendor/friendsofsymfony/user-bundle` directory.

The configuration files

Each application has a need to hold some global and machine-specific parameters and configurations. Symfony2 holds configuration within the `app/config` directory and it is split into a few files as follows:

- `config.yml`
- `config_dev.yml`
- `config_prod.yml`
- `config_test.yml`
- `parameters.yml`

- parameters.yml.dist
- routing.yml
- routing_dev.yml
- security.yml
- services.yml

All the files except the parameters.yml* files contain global configuration, while the parameters.yml file holds machine-specific information such as database host, database name, user, password, and SMTP configuration.

The default configuration file generated by the new Symfony command will be similar to the following one.

This file is auto-generated during the composer install:

```
parameters:
    database_driver: pdo_mysql
    database_host: 127.0.0.1
    database_port: null
    database_name: symfony
    database_user: root
    database_password: null
    mailer_transport: smtp
    mailer_host: 127.0.0.1
    mailer_user: null
    mailer_password: null
    secret: 93b0eebeffd9e229701f74597e10f8ecf4d94d7f
```

As you can see, it mostly holds the parameters related to database, SMTP, locale settings, and secret key that are used internally by Symfony2. Here, you can add your custom parameters using the same syntax. It is a good practice to keep machine-specific data such as passwords, tokens, api-keys, and access keys within this file only. Putting passwords in the general config.yml file is considered as a security risk bug.

The global configuration file (config.yml) is split into a few other files called routing*.yml that contain information about routing on the development and production configuration. The file called as security.yml holds information related to authentication and securing the application access. Note that some files contains information for development, production, or test mode. You can define your mode when you run Symfony through the command-line console and when you run it through the web server. In most cases, while developing you will be using the dev mode.

The Symfony2 console

To finish this chapter, let's take a look at the Symfony console script. We used it before to fire up the development server, but it offers more. Execute the following:

```
$ php app/console
```

You will see a list of supported commands. Each command has a short description. Each of the standard commands come with help, so I will not be describing each of them here, but it is worth to mention a few commonly used ones:

Command	Description
app/console: cache:clear	Symfonys in production uses a lot of caching. Therefore, if you need to change values within a template (Twig) or within configuration files while in production mode, you will need to clear the cache. Cache is also one of the reasons why it's worth to work in the development mode.
app/console container:debug	Displays all configured public services
app/console router:debug	Displays all routing configuration along with method, scheme, host, and path.
app/console security:check	Checks your composer and packages version against known security vulnerabilities. You should run this command regularly.

You can, of course, write your own Symfony2 commands and we will do this within the forthcoming chapters.

Summary

In this chapter, we have demonstrated how to use the Symfony2 installer, test the configuration, run the deployment server, and play around with the Symfony2 command line. We have also installed the composer and learned how to install a package using it.

While we haven't written much code in this chapter, information contained here will be used in all the other chapters. To demonstrate how Symfony2 enables you to make web applications faster, we will try to learn through examples that can be found in real life. To make this task easier, we will try to produce a real to-do web application with modern look and a few working features.

In the next chapter, we will review the default bundle structure, and set up the first routings, controllers, and templates. We will also create some initial database schema and models, and we will present migration and fixtures system.

2
Your First Pages

Most modern PHP frameworks follow a classic MVC concept. Symfony2 is also an MVC framework, so we do have controllers, models, and views. In this chapter, we will learn about these building blocks to see how Symfony2 organizes things:

- Review of the default bundle structure and recommendations
- Setting up the first routings and controllers for the home screen
- Working with templates
- Creating the initial database schema and models
- Loading sample fixtures
- Looking into migration throughout the chapter

Everything is a bundle

In the previous chapter, we dug in to the basic Symfony2 directory structure. Within the `src` directory, we already had two bundles: one called `DemoBundle` within the `Acme` subdirectory and the other one within `AppBundle`.

`DemoBundle` is a showcase of an example bundle that has existed since the beginning of Symfony2. It has been created to demonstrate how Symfony2 organizes things. `AppBundle` is a relatively new thing, introduced in Symfony 2.6 with a new concept of work.

Until the 2.6 version, it was recommended to contain a bundle within the vendor namespace. With Symfony 2.6 and its new best practices rules, it is now recommended to keep the custom application code within the handy `AppBundle` and create other bundles only if you want to create reusable code to be shared among your other projects.

Bundles don't have a fixed directory structure. In fact, you can have a bundle without most of the directories. If you create a utility bundle, it will probably have only some custom directory structure for your own set of libraries and tools and will not contain any of the standard directories.

The standard directories are as follows:

- `Command`: The `Command` directory holds command-line tasks, which are visible when you type:

    ◦ `php app/console`

    ◦ You can see example tasks, and we will create one further in this book

- `Controller`: The `Controller` directory holds the MVC controller classes. You are not limited to a single controller, you can create as many of them as you want. Controllers are our entry classes, and actions within the controllers are called as defined within routing files.

- `Document`: The `Document` directory is used to hold the `Document` files used by **Object Document Mapper (ODM)**. Documents are PHP classes that reflect the MongoDB documents. In future, other document engines may use this, but currently, if you find the `Document` directory in a Symfony2 project there is a great chance that it contains files related to the MongoDB documents.

- `DependencyInjection`: The `DependencyInjection` directory contains a few classes to help in loading bundle services. Usually, if your bundle has its own services (we will discuss this term later in this chapter), you will find some code to load in this directory. It is not required, not every bundle needs services or a special configuration.

- `Form`: The `Form` directory contains classes to handle various HTML forms. Usually, this directory contains a subdirectory with the `Types` and `Subscribers` forms and other helper classes to define, validate, and process various form data.

- `Entity`: The `Entity` directory is similar to the `Document` directory, but it is used to hold entities for SQL databases such as PostgreSQL or MySQL. These files are used by **Doctrine Object Relational Mapper**.

- `Resources`: The `Resources` directory holds non-PHP files related to the bundle. It can be a service definition, routing definition, validation, database entities definition, views, and custom documentation related to the bundle as well as some public files to be copied, or linked to the main web directory.

- `Tests`: The `Tests` directory contains, as you may figure out — classes for automated testing.

You are not limited, and not bound, to use these directories. It is handy to keep the preceding structure as a lot of things are easier this way, but if you want, you can create your own structure. As an example, Symfony2 provides some shortcuts in the `BundleName:ClassName` or `ClassName:actionName` forms, which will work only if you keep a correct structure. Without this, you will be forced to use the full class name (with namespace). This approach is called convention over configuration—you can follow the convention to simplify things, but you can configure it differently if you need to.

There are other standard directory structures that are less common such as `EventListener`, `Service`, and `Twig`, but there are no rules for this. It's up to the developer to choose his own path and structure to organize code.

The configuration format

Symfony2 can handle configuration in different formats: YAML, XML, and annotations. The main configuration files within `app/config` are provided with the YAML format. XML is usually harder to read, and is used only with third-party bundles.

While both YAML and XML configuration are pretty straightforward and need no explanations, we should stop by annotations for a while. As an example, see the `AppBundle/Controller/DefaultController` class:

```
namespace AppBundle\Controller;

use Sensio\Bundle\FrameworkExtraBundle\Configuration\Route;
use Symfony\Bundle\FrameworkBundle\Controller\Controller;

class DefaultController extends Controller
{
    /**
     * @Route("/", name="homepage")
     */
    public function indexAction(Request $request)
    {
        // replace this example code with whatever you need
        return $this->render('default/index.html.twig', array(
            'base_dir' => realpath(
                $this->container
                    ->getParameter('kernel.root_dir').'/..'),
        ));
    }
}
```

If you are familiar with the PHPDoc or JavaDoc convention, you will recognize @token in the preceding example. You may, however, notice one small detail—it's not a standard token. In fact, this token means something; it's not just a comment. In our example, the route annotation (imported through the use keyword here) configures routing with the name homepage and the / URL.

Annotations are usually easy to handle and the most convenient way to configure various aspects of your application but at the same time they are the most controversial.

As you can see, it's handy to have a URL configuration in the same place where the code exists. However, in the case of routing and controllers, it may become hard to navigate over the code, and may cause errors when multiple coders are on board the project.

Some developers avoid annotations because they believe code within comments should not be "parsed", as this is against the idea of having comments. It is worth mentioning that annotations should never be used within the code you want to reuse or keep free from Symfony2 dependencies.

> Within this book, we will be using annotations to configure entity and validation, while using YAML configuration to handle controllers, services, and other configurations. Remember that there is no preferred configuration format. Use the one that feels most comfortable.

Cleanups

Before we start writing our own app, we need to do some cleanups. We need to configure AppBundle to use the YAML configuration. While this is possible to switch the configuration format manually, we will remove the bundle (it doesn't contain much code yet), and we will generate a new bundle to demonstrate new bundle creation.

Recreating AppBundle

To recreate AppBundle, remove it first as follows:

```
$ rm -rf src/AppBundle
```

Remove it from app/AppKernel.php by removing the following line:

```
    new AppBundle\AppBundle(),
```

Remove it's routing (app/config/routing.yml), which is as follows:

```
app:
    resource: @AppBundle/Controller/
    type:     annotation
```

Now we will need to generate it again. Issue the following command:

```
$ php app/console generate:bundle --namespace=AppBundle
```

Now provide the following answers to the generator:

```
Bundle name [AppBundle]: [Enter]

Target directory [.../todoapp/src]: [Enter]

Configuration format (yml, xml, php, or annotation): yml

Do you want to generate the whole directory structure [no]? [Enter]

Do you confirm generation [yes]? [Enter]

Confirm automatic update of your Kernel [yes]? [Enter]

Confirm automatic update of the Routing [yes]? [Enter]
```

So basically, we want all the options to be default ones, and we will choose the YAML configuration to use.

After a successful generation, look into app/config/routing.yml. You will notice a slight change in this routing:

```
app:
    resource: "@AppBundle/Resources/config/routing.yml"
    prefix:   /
```

As it does not use annotations now and routing is handled through traditional YAML files, it has some advantages, the most obvious one — you keep your AppBundle routing information in a single file rather than place it in various controllers and actions.

You will note more directories in the created bundle. As we are using the YAML format now, we also got the services.yml file within the Resources/config file, and we have the DependencyInjection directory with two files created.

There is also one more change, look into the controller. It is much shorter now:

```
namespace AppBundle\Controller;

use Symfony\Bundle\FrameworkBundle\Controller\Controller;

class DefaultController extends Controller
```

```
{
    public function indexAction($name)
    {
        return $this->render('AppBundle:Default:index.html.twig',
            array('name' => $name));
    }
}
```

The routing annotation is gone; action code seems much cleaner now. You may also notice a slight difference within the `indexAction` method. The method now gets a parameter and returns it in an array. The `render` argument has also been slightly changed. To explain this change in the parameters of the method, we need to dive into routing.

Routing

Like with many other frameworks based on the concept of MVC, before any controller is actually executed, Symfony2 needs to know how to handle it. The Symfony routing configuration starts within the `app/config/routing_*.yml` file. Depending on which environment you fire up, this version of routing is fired up. Usually, this environment file loads the main `app/config/routing.yml` file, which loads other files from vendors, bundles, and so on. You can, of course, directly define your own single routings here, but it's usually recommended to keep the bundle-specific routings within the bundle itself, while using the main routing only to import resources.

As per the example provided earlier in this chapter, we know our app tries to import another resource file defined as `@AppBundle/Resources/config/routing.yml`. The `@BundleName` syntax is a shortcut to the bundle namespace (in our case `AppBundle`) but namespace can be longer if you include the vendor in your name. Let's take a look at the bundle routing by looking into the `src/AppBundle/Resources/config/routing.yml` file. You will see something similar to this:

```
app_homepage:
    path:     /hello/{name}
    defaults: { _controller: AppBundle:Default:index }
```

Here, `app_homepage` is our routing name. When you want to generate a URL within a view, or when you want to redirect to a URL you will need to use the routing name to let the framework know which URL you want to generate and what parameters it should expect.

If you create a reusable bundle, it is a good habit to prefix your routing to avoid conflicts, but when you create your app routing, you can actually create them as short as possible, to make it easier for you to handle and make reference to. Just make sure you are not using the same name twice, as this will overwrite one of the rules.

Parameters are enclosed within curly brackets, so in our case, we define a URL /hello/{name} with a static part, /hello/, and a dynamic part, {name}. The dynamic part can be anything; it just needs to be properly encoded into the URL.

You may also notice the controller is referenced in an unusual way, without specifying the full path within the namespace. It's because Symfony assumes that the controller lies within the Controller directory of the selected bundle, and this allows you to use short syntax. The long one would be as follows: AppBundle\Controller\DefaultController::indexAction.

You can also provide default values to make your parameter optional. Let's modify this file a bit:

```
hello:
    path:      /hello/{name}
    defaults: { _controller: AppBundle:Default:index, name:
'anonymous' }
```

We changed the name of routing to hello, and provided a default value for the name parameter. Now it's time to look at how our code change is working. Call your project URL, http://127.0.0.1:8000/hello. You should see a **Hello anonymous!** welcome text. If you type http://127.0.0.1:8000/hello/john, you will see a **Hello john!** message.

 If you don't see the code under the URL, make sure that your server is up and running and listening on this port. Go back to *Chapter 1, The Symfony Framework – Installation and Configuration*, if you need any more help.

We should look back at our controller code, as it needs more explanation. Let's focus on the action method:

```
public function indexAction($name)
{
    return $this->render('AppBundle:Default:index.html.twig',
        array('name' => $name));
}
```

There are a few rules for methods within the controller to follow:

- Only action methods should be `public`
- Controller methods should be short; if your controller is long, consider refactoring it
- Action methods must have the `Action` suffix
- Action methods should return a valid response object

To return a response, you can do the following:

- Render a template through the helper render method
- Create a response object

Usually, when we deal with templates, we will use the helper method, however if the response is not HTML, but JSON or URL redirection, we don't need to rely on helper methods, creating a new object of `RedirectResponse()` or `JsonResponse()`.

> Note that these classes exist within the Symfony framework `Symfony\Component\HttpFoundation` namespace.

The `render()` helper accepts a few parameters. The first is a template name. When we created the project, the template name was `default/index.html.twig` and with the new bundle, it is called `AppBundle:Default:index.html.twig`. The difference is in the location of the template. The first one is located within the main `app/Resources/views` directory, the second one exists within our bundle's `src/AppBundle/Resources/views` directory. It is recommended to have application templates within `app/Resources/views`, since this gives you shorter syntax. It's totally up to you which version you choose.

> Templates within this book will be created within `app/Resources/views`.

Templates – the View layer

Each MVC framework offers the View layer, and Symfony2 is no different. In Symfony1, we were using plain PHP code. Symfony has introduced a new templating engine named Twig. The Symfony syntax is more elegant — it's shorter and designed to be cleaner than regular PHP code in templates.

We can still use it now. However, it's not the recommended approach, as in most cases, you will not find examples of a working bundle code in pure PHP.

Let's take a look at the template code within our bundle, `src/AppBundle/Resources/views/Default/index.html.twig`:

```
Hello {{ name }}!
```

Yes, this is it. As you can figure out, `{{ name }}` outputs the variable name. It is an equivalent of `<?php echo $name; ?>`. The code actually doesn't do much, and it is not a valid HTML code (it just outputs some text). Let's modify it a little:

```
{% extends '::base.html.twig' %}

{% block body %}
Hello {{ name }}!
{% endblock body %}
```

Now try to fire `http://127.0.0.1:8000/app_dev.php/hello/john` in the browser.

The change is subtle, but now the code renders a correct HTML code with all proper tags, and as a bonus, in the development mode, you get a Debug toolbar at the bottom.

So let's explain what we've done so far. In the first line, we used extends, which means that our template, just like class, extends after another one. The syntax to call the template is the same as within the controller, with one exception. If we want to call for the template within `app/Resources/view`, we need to use the `::` double colon prefix. Note that it's enclosed within `{% … %}`. These characters indicate control structure. A control structure does not output code directly, it is used to control the flow. For example, the `if` statement, loops, setting new variables, and so on.

When we extend the syntax, we can't place the new code anywhere. We need to let the parent template know which fragment we want to override. We do this by using blocks.

Let's take a look at the base template in `app/Resources/views/base.html.twig`:

```
<!DOCTYPE html>
<html>
    <head>
        <meta charset="UTF-" />
        <title>{% block title %}Welcome!{% endblock %}</title>
```

```
        {% block stylesheets %}{% endblock %}
        <link rel="icon" type="image/x-icon" href="{{ asset('favicon.
ico') }}" />
    </head>
    <body>
        {% block body %}{% endblock %}
        {% block javascripts %}{% endblock %}
    </body>
</html>
```

This is pretty much a standard HTML code, but with a few Twig blocks defined: `title`, `stylesheets`, `body`, and `javascript`. Most of these are empty now, and we will fill these over time.

As you may have noticed, within our `index.html.twig` file, we have replaced the body block with the new content.

 You may wonder how the Debug toolbar gets injected. This is done through adding the Debug toolbar's code just before the `</body>` tag. If you remove the body tag from the template, you will not get the debug toolbar. It means the Debug toolbar will not be rendered on non-HTML pages.

We will deal with Twig and templates more deeply in the next chapter, focusing just on the View layer. It is worth remembering that views should not be complicated and should not contain complicated logic. It's not their job.

 Note that if you alter the Twig template, to see your changes you need to either work in development mode or clear the cache. In the production mode, templates are compiled in to PHP files, so changes are not reflected until you refresh the cache. If you want to clear the cache, refer to the list of common command-line commands in the first chapter.

Entities – the Model layer

Finally, we need to dive into the Model layer of Symfony2 framework. Symfony2 heavily relies on Doctrine2. Doctrine2 is one of the most popular object-relational mapping libraries. While there are alternatives like Propel, in many cases most of the third-party bundles support only Doctrine2.

To create a database model, we need to properly connect to the database first. Make sure that the `properties.yml` file contains the correct values, and you are able to connect to your database.

 Note that in the production mode, each change within the YAML file requires the cache to be cleared, otherwise, it will not be noticed. In the development mode, the configuration is recreated without this requirement.

Now, we need to create our first entity file. In case of entities, we will use annotation as this seems the easiest way to handle database changes and migrations. This will also make it easier for us to make changes in the future and add other stuff related to entity-like validation or file handlers.

Now we will create files to hold tags and tasks for our to-do app. We will start with tags. Create a new file in the `src/AppBundle/Entity` directory (create one if it does not exist) called `Tag.php`, and fill it with the following code:

```php
<?php

namespace AppBundle\Entity;

use Doctrine\ORM\Mapping as ORM;

/**
 * @ORM\Entity
 * @ORM\Table(name="todo_tag")
 */
class Tag
{
    /**
     * @ORM\Id
     * @ORM\Column(type="integer")
     * @ORM\GeneratedValue(strategy="AUTO")
     */
    private $id;

    /**
     * @ORM\Column(type="string", length=255)
     */
    private $name;
}
```

You don't need to generate getters and setters; Symfony2 offers a command-line generator for this. We will use this later in the chapter. To make an entity, we need to let Symfony2 and Doctrine know that we have an entity. To make this possible, we are importing the Doctrine annotation as follows:

```
use Doctrine\ORM\Mapping as ORM;
```

Now we mark the class as an entity using the `@ORM\Entity` reference. The `@ORM\Table` reference allows us to define the table name, but also sets up the column indexes and unique indexes. Before adding the variables, we are adding the annotation to define their database type and properties:

```
/**
 * @ORM\Id
 * @ORM\Column(type="integer")
 * @ORM\GeneratedValue(strategy="AUTO")
 */
private $id;
```

The preceding code defines the required primary key and integer. Values will be generated automatically using database engine options (in case of MySQL, it's auto-increment).

The property is as follows:

```
/**
 * @ORM\Column(type="string", length=255)
 */
private $name;
```

This defines the `name` column and the type of string (string type will be translated to `varchar`) of `length=255`. This is also a required value.

Now let's focus on creating a task entity:

```
<?php

namespace AppBundle\Entity;

use Doctrine\ORM\Mapping as ORM;

/**
 * @ORM\Entity
 * @ORM\Table(name="todo_task")
 */
class Task
```

```
{
    /**
     * @ORM\Id
     * @ORM\Column(type="integer")
     * @ORM\GeneratedValue(strategy="AUTO")
     */
    private $id;

    /**
     * @ORM\ManyToMany(targetEntity="Tag")
     */
    private $tags;

    /**
     * @ORM\Column(type="string", length=255)
     */
    private $name;

    /**
     * @ORM\Column(type="text", nullable=true)
     */
    private $notes;

    /**
     * @ORM\Column(type="date", nullable=true)
     */
    private $due_date;

    /**
     * @ORM\Column(type="datetime")
     */
    private $created_at;
}
```

This is similar to the previous one — it contains all the @ORM\Entity, @ORM\Table, and other annotations. The new one here is an annotation for the text type, date, and the datetime type (this will be translated into the PHP DateTime class). Note that the due_date column is optional, as it does allow null values.

The last and interesting thing here is the definition of the relation:

```
    /**
     * @ORM\ManyToMany(targetEntity="Tag")
     */
    private $tags;
```

This will create an M:N relationship between the tags and tasks, allowing the tasks to have multiple tags. There are also other kind of relations—ManyToOne, OneToMany, and OneToOne, to reflect N:1, 1:N, and 1:1 relations. You can read about them in the official Doctrine documentation under `http://doctrine-orm.readthedocs.org/en/latest/reference/association-mapping.html`.

After we have created these values, we should validate them. Type the following:

```
$ php app/console doctrine:schema:validate
```

The result should be similar to the following:

```
[Mapping]  OK - The mapping files are correct.
[Database] FAIL - The database schema is not in sync with the current
mapping file.
```

While it will show that the database is not yet synced, the mapping should be correct. Note that the properties created within our class have a private status. It's intentional, we should avoid creating public variables within an entity, and we should keep entities as simple as possible.

Now we should generate the getters/setters. Type the following command:

```
$ php app/console doctrine:generate:entities --no-backup AppBundle
```

You should see something similar to the following:

```
Generating entities for bundle "AppBundle"
  > generating AppBundle\Entity\Tag
  > generating AppBundle\Entity\Task
```

If you look at your entities again, you will notice that they contain getters and setters now.

> The generator will not override your code, so it's usually safe to use the `no-backup` option. If you are uncertain, you can skip it and use the default backup behavior. The generator will then back up your entities before altering them and save them, with the ~ suffix, in the same location where the original files are.

To generate the SQL code, type the following:

```
$ php app/console doctrine:schema:update --dump-sql
```

You should see the SQL definitions for the tables we just created:

```
$ php app/console doctrine:schema:update --force
```

This will result in the following database update:

```
Updating database schema...
Database schema updated successfully! "5" queries were executed
```

Migrations

While the `update` method will suit your needs in most cases, you may need to use more sophisticated solutions. If you do have such needs, you should look into `DoctrineMigrationsBundle`, which is not a part of Symfony, but it can be downloaded and installed through packagist.

The migrations bundle offers some more advanced features such as:

- Allows you to modify the SQL code used for migration
- Ability to rollback your changes
- Ability to manually run a single version of migration

Fixtures

After creating the database structure, it would be handy to prepare some test data. We can do this through fixtures. Unfortunately, Symfony2 does not come with any fixtures system, so we need to install it. Type the following:

$ php composer.phar require doctrine/doctrine-fixtures-bundle

Now register the bundle in `app/AppKernel.php`:

```
class AppKernel extends Kernel
{
    public function registerBundles()
    {
        $bundles = array(
        // […]
        if (in_array(/* […] */, array('dev', 'test'))) {
            // ...
        $bundles[] = new Doctrine\Bundle\FixturesBundle\
DoctrineFixturesBundle();
}
```

If everything goes well, you should see new options when you type the following:

$ php app/console

This should give you a new command called `doctrine:fixtures:load`.

Now let's create a simple fixture class to load an example tag.

In the `src/AppBundle/DataFixtures/ORM` directory, create a file called `LoadTagData.php`:

```php
<?php

namespace AppBundle\DataFixtures\ORM;

use Doctrine\Common\DataFixtures\FixtureInterface;
use Doctrine\Common\Persistence\ObjectManager;
use AppBundle\Entity\Tag;

class LoadUserData implements FixtureInterface
{
    public function load(ObjectManager $manager)
    {
        $tags = ['company', 'home', 'important'];

        foreach ($tags as $tag) {
            $obj = new Tag();
            $obj->setName($tag);
            $manager->persist($obj);
        }

        $manager->flush();
    }
}
```

Now you should execute this using the following command:

```
$ php app/console doctrine:fixtures:load
```

You should see something similar to the following:

```
Careful, database will be purged. Do you want to continue Y/N ? y
  > purging database
  > loading AppBundle\DataFixtures\ORM\LoadUserData
```

This loads the fixtures data to our database. It is possible to create more sophisticated fixtures, use a container, change the load order, and so on. We will create more advanced fixtures in the forthcoming chapters.

Summary

In this chapter, we got a quick overview of the Symfony bundle structure, and we looked at the way Symfony2 handles MVC pattern. We also started creating our to-do app by defining the database model and adding some fixtures data.

In the next chapter, we will dig deeper into the Twig system, create assets, install the `css/javascript` semantic UI framework, and we will prepare our to-do list view filled with some example tasks.

Twig Templating and Assets Handling

When you look into PHP, you may notice that over the last years the language has evolved, more mature concepts and design patterns have been created, and the approach to create the output has also changed drastically. Symfony2 as a modern framework tries to give you modern tools to make frontend development easier. In this chapter, we will cover the following topics:

- The Twig templating engine
- Assets management
- Installing the frontend library
- Adding advanced fixtures

The Twig templating engine

When Symfony1 was created, the framework did not use any of existing template systems but relied on just the PHP as a template language. It had some advantages (that is, templates did not require any processing and were very fast), but wasn't too friendly for frontend developers. Also, PHP is a very verbose language and you need to write a lot of code to do some basic stuff such as checking a variable and determining whether it exists or is empty. Also, escaping variables requires some coding.

In Symfony2, a new templating engine, called Twig, was introduced. Twig was written with a few concepts in mind, such as:

- **Templating system is extensible**: Developer may write their own extensions to it very easily.

- **Fast**: The written template is compiled and processed, generating an optimized PHP code on the output.
- **More secure**: It is much easier to make code secure using Twig with features such as auto-escape or sandboxing.
- **Optimized for frontend development**: The Twig syntax has been optimized to make frontend development quicker and more convenient by providing shortcuts for commonly used patterns (loops, default variable values, and so on).

As usual with Symfony2, using Twig is optional but it is recommended. While the basic framework has the support for simple PHP templating, most of the extensions available in the open source community embraced Twig, and their authors don't bother with providing working examples without Twig.

 If you want to find more information about Twig, please visit its home page at http://twig.sensiolabs.org/.

Assets management

In every large web project, you will need to use images, CSS, and JS files. Usually these files are not generated dynamically, but saved statically and served by the HTTP server, so the templating system in this case is not very useful.

Within Symfony2, there were a few different ways to help with this:

- Managing assets from bundles by installing them on the public web/ directory
- Generating a combined CSS/JS file through Assetic

Assetic

Assetic is a tool that allows you to manipulate assets files (javascripts, css) and process them before they are served to the browser. This allows you to have your own "development" versions of your files, while serving to the browser a minified, compressed, and combined version of the files.

Assetic handles its job through filters. In the following example, see the default configuration example stored in config.yml:

```
# Assetic Configuration
assetic:
```

```
debug:          "%kernel.debug%"
use_controller: false
bundles:        [ ]
#java: /usr/bin/java
filters:
    cssrewrite: ~
    #closure:
    #    jar: "%kernel.root_dir%/Resources/java/compiler.jar"
    #yui_css:
    #    jar: "%kernel.root_dir%/Resources/java/yuicompressor-
2.4.7.jar"
```

The default setup uses the `cssrewrite` filter. This filter is responsible for setting up correct relative paths when working with bundles. You can also define your own filters such as the Less and Sass compiler.

A detailed configuration of Assetic is not within the scope of this book. If you seek more information about this, see the official documentation at `https://symfony.com/doc/current/cookbook/assetic/index.html`.

Handling third-party bundle assets

When you install a third-party bundle, it often comes with its own CSS, JS, or other files such as fonts and images. Within Symfony2, you can "install" such files on the public directory by issuing the following command:

```
$ php app/console assets:install –symlink
```

This command will try to create `symlink` or copy assets to the `web/bundles` directory. After this, our assets will be available under a normalized bundle name within the `web/bundles` directory. The normalized name contains only lowercase letters and does not contain the word "bundle". So for example, `AcmeDemoBundle` will be converted to `acmedemo`.

> The `--symlink` option is useful on the *nix systems, as it creates only a symbolic link to an assets directory, which not only saves time but also sometimes makes development easier. It is not supported on Windows systems.

The same mechanism also works for your assets, which are placed in the bundle. If you create any file or directory in the `src/AppBundle/Resources/public` directory, it will be installed on `web/bundles/app`.

Handling your application assets

In your project, you will probably use a lot of JS and CSS files, which are not part of any Symfony2 bundle, such as jQuery, Bootstrap, or something else. As of Symfony 2.6, there is a recommendation to install these files directly on the `web/` directory rather than using bundles. Also, it is recommended to write your own CSS/JS files here rather than putting files in various places and bundles.

Since writing tons of CSS and JavaScript is not in the scope of this book, we will use a UI component framework called semantic UI.

Go to `http://1.semantic-ui.com/` and download the latest version 1 release. At the time this book was written, the current stable version of Semantic UI was 1.12.0. After you download the file, unpack it and copy the following files and directories from `dist/`:

```
themes/ -> web/css/vendor/semantic-ui/themes
semantic.min.css -> web/css/vendor/semantic-ui
semantic.min.js -> web/js/vendor/semantic-ui
```

Our own styles will be placed in the files that will be placed in `web/css/dev/app.css` and `web/js/dev/app.js`, so create them (they are empty for now).

After you do this, your `web/css` directory should contain the following:

```
dev/app.css
vendor/semantic-ui/themes/ (and subdirectories)
vendor/semantic-ui/semantic.min.css
```

The `web/js` directory should contain the following:

```
web/js/dev/app.js
web/js/vendor/semantic-ui/semantic.min.js
```

Now, we need to configure our project to handle these files, and we need to link these files to our page. Unless you are using some fancy frontend tool, such as Grunt, you may use Assetic to do the job.

Before we show how to use this, first we need to create a new controller to handle the tasks list. We will start by creating a new template. Create a new directory and file under `app/Resources/views/task/list.html.twig` with the following content:

```twig
{% extends '::base.html.twig' %}

{% block body %}
    <h2 class="ui aligned header">Your tasks list</h2>
    <p class="ui aligned">
```

```
        Below you will find your unfinished tasks
    </p>
{% endblock %}
```

The preceding code will be displayed on our homepage. Now we need to create a new controller and routing entry. Add the following code:

```php
<?php

// file: src/AppBundle/Controller/TaskController.php
namespace AppBundle\Controller;

use Symfony\Bundle\FrameworkBundle\Controller\Controller;
use Symfony\Component\HttpFoundation\Request;

class TaskController extends Controller
{
    public function listAction(Request $request)
    {
        return $this->render('task/list.html.twig');
    }
}
```

Now modify the src/AppBundle/Resources/config/routing.yml file by replacing its content with the following:

```
homepage:
    path:    /
    defaults: { _controller: AppBundle:Task:list }
```

When you see your page at http://127.0.0.1:8000/, you should see a basic browser styling as we haven't added the style sheets yet.

Now go to app/Resources/base.html.twig and modify the blocks responsible for JS and CSS. The complete code should look as follows:

```twig
<!DOCTYPE html>
<html>
    <head>
        <meta charset="UTF-8" />
        <title>{% block title %}Welcome!{% endblock %}</title>
        {% block stylesheets %}
            {% stylesheets
                'css/vendor/semantic-ui/semantic.min.css'
                'css/dev/app.css'
                filter='cssrewrite'
                output='css/app.css'
```

```
            %}
                <link rel="stylesheet" href="{{ asset_url }}" />
            {% endstylesheets %}
        {% endblock %}
        <link rel="icon" type="image/x-icon" href="{{ asset('favicon.
ico') }}" />
    </head>
    <body>
        {% block body %}{% endblock %}
        {% block javascripts %}
            <script src="https://ajax.googleapis.com/ajax/libs/
jquery/2.1.3/jquery.min.js"></script>
            {% javascripts
                'js/vendor/semantic-ui/semantic.min.js'
                'js/dev/app.js'
                output='js/app.js'
            %}
                <script src="{{ asset_url }}"></script>
            {% endjavascripts %}
        {% endblock %}
    </body>
</html>
```

As you may have noticed in the javascripts and stylesheets blocks, we have used Assetic commands. For both JS and CSS, it accepts a list of files as parameters and generates an output file when you issue the following command:

$ php app/console assetic:dump --env=prod

This command will generate the following two files specified by the output parameter:

```
Dumping all prod assets.
Debug mode is off.

... /app/../web/css/app.css
... /app/../web//js/app.js
```

Now when you look at your css and js directories, you will notice new combined files. This way we don't have to include multiple css/js files but just one. Also, note the parameter within the stylesheets block containing the cssrewrite filter. This filter is responsible for rewriting relative paths within the css file to the correct location, so you don't have to worry whether your development css file or vendor file will loose its relative path to images or fonts, as this filter will amend the paths to the correct ones.

It would be very slow if we have to execute this command with every new file change. Fortunately, the Assetic manager in the development mode will be using Symfony2 for dynamic generation of new files and will notice any changes in the included files, without a need to dump assets.

 If you run a standalone server, you work in the development mode by default, so you don't have to worry about dumping, but remember this before deploying your work on the production environment.

After you modify your main template, refresh it. You would notice a slight change in the fonts of your header and text. It now looks more polished, but still sticks to the edges of page. Modify `web/css/dev/app.css`, and add the following code:

```
body {
  padding: 25px;
}
```

Refresh your homepage. You should see the visual changes.

 Assetic has a lot more options. Instead of just `cssrewrite`, it can help you to minimize files but it does not come with these filters built-in, so using them usually requires installing some extra tools.

Now we will remove leftovers from the previously created default controller and views. Remove the following files:

```
app/Resources/views/default/index.html.twig
src/AppBundle/Controller/DefaultController.php
src/AppBundle/Resources/views/Default/index.html.twig
```

Empty all directories, and then clear the cache:

```
$ php app/console cache:clear
```

Creating a list of tasks

After we are set, we should create a table with a list of our unfinished tasks. In the previous chapter, when we created a database model we didn't add a column to flag the finished task, so we will do this now to demonstrate how the database model should be amended while the project is growing.

Modify the `src/AppBundle/Entity/Task.php` file and add the following:

```php
// ...
/**
 * @ORM\Column(type="datetime")
 */
private $created_at;

// add the code below, to recognize finished tasks:
/**
 * @ORM\Column(type="boolean")
 */
private $finished = false;
```

Update the database and generate the following new methods:

```
$ php app/console doctrine:schema:update --force
$ php app/console doctrine:generate:entities --no-backup AppBundle
```

Now we need to modify our data fixtures. In the previous chapter, we created an example tag fixture, now we need to add an example task. Add the following code to the file:

```php
<?php

// file: src/AppBundle/DataFixtures/ORM/LoadTaskData.php
namespace AppBundle\DataFixtures\ORM;

use AppBundle\Entity\Task;
use Doctrine\Common\DataFixtures\FixtureInterface;
use Doctrine\Common\Persistence\ObjectManager;

class LoadTaskData implements FixtureInterface
{
    public function load(ObjectManager $manager)
    {
        $obj = new Task();
        $obj->setName('Example task for today');
        $obj->setNotes('This task is created as a fixture and has no
real meaning. It\'s only demonstration, sorry to disappoint you');
        $obj->setCreatedAt(new \DateTime());
        $obj->setFinished(false);

        $manager->persist($obj);
```

```
        $manager->flush();
    }
}
```

Load the new data as follows:

$ php app/console doctrine:fixtures:load

The preceding code will simply load a new task to the database.

Now we need to modify the controller to read the tasks list from the database. Modify src/AppBundle/Controller/TaskController.php as follows:

```
    public function listAction(Request $request)
    {
        $em = $this->getDoctrine()->getManager();

        $tasks = $em->getRepository('AppBundle:Task')
            ->createQueryBuilder('t')
            ->where('t.finished = :finished')
            ->orderBy('t.due_date', 'ASC')
            ->setParameter('finished', false)
            ->getQuery()
            ->getResult();

        return $this->render('task/list.html.twig', ['tasks' =>
$tasks]);
    }
```

What we have changed here is that we used entity manager and created an SQL query using query builder. In this query, we have requested for all entities that have the finished status set to false. We also requested our data to be sorted out by the due_date column. The result of the database query is then passed to the template.

Finally, we need to implement the view. Edit app/Resources/views/task/list.html.twig so it looks like the following:

```
    {% extends '::base.html.twig' %}

    {% block body %}
        <h2 class="ui aligned header">Your tasks list</h2>
        <p class="ui aligned">Below you will find your unfinished tasks</
p>

        <table class="ui blue table">
```

```
<thead>
    <tr>
        <th>Name</th>
        <th>Notes</th>
        <th>Tags</th>
        <th>Due</th>
    </tr>
</thead>
<tbody>
    {% for task in tasks %}
    <tr>
        <td>{{ task.name }}</td>
        <td>{{ task.notes }}</td>
        <td>
            {% for tag in task.tags %}
            <span class="ui tag label">{{ tag.name }}</span>
            {% endfor %}
        </td>
        <td>
            {{ task.dueDate is empty ? "" : task.
dueDate|date('Y-m-d') }}
        </td>
    </tr>
    {% else %}
        <tr>
            <td colspan="4" class="center aligned">
                    <h2>There are no unfinished tasks at the
moment. Good Job!</h2>
            </td>
        </tr>
    {% endfor %}
</tbody>
    </table>
{% endblock %}
```

The most interesting part of the code is highlighted. As you may have observed, the for...end loop can also have a default value in case the if loop is empty and provided with a simple else keyword. This is very convenient when you need to provide an elegant default value for situations where the provided array is empty.

The next interesting thing is the way Twig handles the objects and arrays. When reaching for task.name in a PHP object, Twig, in fact, is looking for the getName or isName method, and when such a method exists, it will be used. If you provide an array and not an object, Twig will look for the name key and will use its value.

Another interesting thing happens around the `dueDate` method. Doctrine ORM for every date and time column transforms data using the standard PHP `DateTime` object. As we cannot just output the object, we need to use the Twig filter. With Twig we are using filter very often, it's one of the basic ways to modify a provided variable. In our case, we are checking whether the date provided to our object is null, and if not, we will format it using the PHP `DateTime` method format syntax to display date in the YYYY-MM-DD format.

When you finish everything, you will probably have results similar to this one:

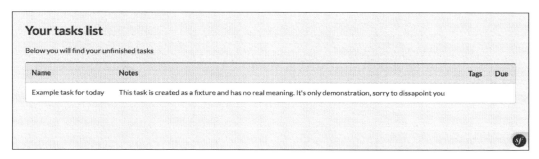

You may have noticed that both the tags and due fields are empty. It's because we didn't connect our tags and task in fixtures, and we left the due date field empty.

In order to add tags to the task object, we need to slightly modify our fixtures. First, modify the `src/AppBundle/DataFixtures/ORM/LoadTagData.php` file:

```php
<?php

namespace AppBundle\DataFixtures\ORM;

use Doctrine\Common\DataFixtures\AbstractFixture;
use Doctrine\Common\DataFixtures\OrderedFixtureInterface;
use Doctrine\Common\Persistence\ObjectManager;
use AppBundle\Entity\Tag;

class LoadTagData extends AbstractFixture implements
OrderedFixtureInterface
{
    public function load(ObjectManager $manager)
    {
        // ... code written in previous chapter
        $manager->persist($obj);

        // adding object as reference, to use it later
```

```
        $this->addReference('tag:'.$tag, $obj);
        // ...
    }

    public function getOrder()
    {
        return 1;
    }
}
```

The highlighted updates to the code add the `Tag` objects to the reference table and allows to fetch the object when it's needed. In our case, our references will be called `tag:company`, `tag:home`, or `tag:important`. When we are adding references, the order of objects loaded is important, so we are also implementing `OrderedFixtureInterface` and a simple method to inform Doctrine in what order it should load the files.

Similar updates need to be added to `src/AppBundle/DataFixtures/ORM/LoadTaskData.php`:

```
use Doctrine\Common\DataFixtures\AbstractFixture;
use Doctrine\Common\DataFixtures\OrderedFixtureInterface;
use AppBundle\Entity\Task;
use Doctrine\Common\Persistence\ObjectManager;

class LoadTaskData extends AbstractFixture implements
OrderedFixtureInterface
{
    public function load(ObjectManager $manager)
    {
        // ...
        $obj->setDueDate(new \DateTime());
        $obj->addTag($this->getReference('tag:home'));
        $obj->addTag($this->getReference('tag:important'));

        $manager->persist($obj);
        $manager->flush();
    }

    public function getOrder()
    {
        return 10;
    }
}
```

In this class, we are adding a method to mark the load order, but we are also getting tags as referenced objects. Now we need to reload the data as follows:

```
$ php app/console doctrine:fixtures:load
```

Now we are done.

 As we have used only one filter in this chapter, we will use more of them in the following chapters. If you are interested and want to learn more about them, go to the Twig documentation at http://twig.sensiolabs.org/doc/filters/index.html.

Summary

In this chapter, we learned how to write more sophisticated templates, iterate over objects fetched from database, and install and configure external `stylesheets` and `javascript` libraries.

In the next chapter, we will take a closer look at forms, data processing, and validation.

4
Forms

Forms handling, processing, and validation are some of the most common things that we do when we create a web application, and practically, the only way we can request data from a website visitor or user. Handling forms effectively was always one of the most requested features in all modern frameworks. In this chapter, we will go deeply into the process of form creation, validation, and saving data.

Form creation

Symfony2 uses the form component to make the creation of forms easier. The form component is a standalone library and can be used independently, but integration with Symfony2 is very good and seamless.

We have two ways to generate forms. The quicker one is to define forms directly within the controller. While this is the quickest way to create a form, it is not the most elegant one. Forms created in this way are not easy to refactor and are not reusable.

For example, to add a new task to our list, we could define the following form in our task controller in `src/AppBundle/Controller/TaskController.php`:

```php
<?php

namespace AppBundle\Controller;

use AppBundle\Entity\Task;
use Symfony\Bundle\FrameworkBundle\Controller\Controller;
use Symfony\Component\HttpFoundation\Request;

class TaskController extends Controller
{
    public function listAction(Request $request)
```

```
        {
            $em = $this->getDoctrine()->getManager();

            $tasks = $em->getRepository('AppBundle:Task')
                ->createQueryBuilder('t')
                ->where('t.finished = :finished')
                ->orderBy('t.due_date', 'ASC')
                ->setParameter('finished', false)
                ->getQuery()
                ->getResult();

            $newTask = new Task();

            $form = $this->createFormBuilder($newTask)
                ->add('name', 'text')
                ->add('notes', 'text')
                ->add('dueDate', 'date')
                ->add('add', 'submit', ['label' => 'Add Task'])
                ->getForm();

            return $this->render('task/list.html.twig', [
                'tasks' => $tasks,
                'form' => $form->createView()
            ]);
        }
    }
```

Our next step is to set up some default values. The easiest way to add some default values is to add them to the entity constructor. Add the following code to src/AppBundle/Entity/Task.php:

```
/**
 * @ORM\Entity
 * @ORM\Table(name="todo_task")
 */
class Task
{
    /* ... */

    /**
     * Constructor
     */
    public function __construct()
    {
```

```
        // tags value is auto-generated
        $this->tags = new \Doctrine\Common\Collections\
ArrayCollection();

        // adding default values
        $this->due_date = new \DateTime('+1 day');
        $this->created_at = new \DateTime();
        $this->finished = false;
    }
```

In our view in app/Resources/views/task/list.html.twig, we can simply add the following:

```
{% extends '::base.html.twig' %}

{% block body %}
    {# ... table defined in previous chapter #}
    </table>

    <p>New task:</p>
    {{ form(form) }}
{% endblock %}
```

Now, when you refresh your page, below the list of tasks you should see the new form element. The preceding code created a new form type within the controller, and we used form Twig helper to render the whole form at once.

Note that this way of rendering a form as presented in the preceding code snippet is very easy, but not very flexible. We will discuss more options to render forms further in this chapter.

This approach is simple, though it's often better to create a separate form. It is not recommended to have huge controller classes. Also, separating a form makes it easier to refactor and reuse the code in future.

Now let's try to create the same form, but in a more elegant way. In Symfony2, these form classes are called form types and usually, are placed in Form\Type within the bundle. Let's create a new file, src/AppBundle/Form/Type/TaskType.php, with the following content:

```
<?php

namespace AppBundle\Form\Type;
```

```php
use Symfony\Component\Form\AbstractType;
use Symfony\Component\Form\FormBuilderInterface;
use Symfony\Component\OptionsResolver\OptionsResolver;

class TaskType extends AbstractType
{
    public function buildForm(
        FormBuilderInterface $builder, array $options
    ) {

        $builder
            ->add('name')
            ->add('notes')
            ->add('due_date')
            ->add('add', 'submit', ['label' => 'Add Task'])
        ;

    }

    public function configureOptions(OptionsResolver $resolver)
    {
        $resolver->setDefaults([
            'data_class' => 'AppBundle\Entity\Task',
        ]);
    }

    public function getName()
    {
        return 'task';
    }

}
```

This is basically the same form that we created previously. There are a few differences, though:

- The form type class needs to have a getName method to define the form namespace. This value will be used to contain form fields within this namespace.

- We can set up default options within such a class. Here, we can define the data class (the class used to serialize data into, or define some form options like CSRF protection or validation groups).

The buildForm method, as you can see, is very similar to the methods we created. You may notice that we do not define the type of fields. This has happened because they were guessed from the entity field type.

To use this class, we need to slightly change our controller class, as follows:

```php
<?php

namespace AppBundle\Controller;

use AppBundle\Entity\Task;
use AppBundle\Form\Type\TaskType;
use Symfony\Bundle\FrameworkBundle\Controller\Controller;
use Symfony\Component\HttpFoundation\Request;

class TaskController extends Controller
{
    public function listAction(Request $request)
    {
        $em = $this->getDoctrine()->getManager();

        /../

        $newTask = new Task();

        $form = $this->createForm(new TaskType(), $newTask);

        return $this->render('task/list.html.twig', [
            'tasks' => $tasks,
            'form' => $form->createView()
        ]);
    }
}
```

In the preceding code, we replaced the code of the form with the newly created form type. All the other things remain the same, including displaying the types.

If you want to create a form type based on array data and not based on entity, you can, of course, do this simply by not defining a data class and passing an array of values instead of an entity object. In this case, you will have to define the type of the field.

Symfony2 has a lot of built-in types. The text fields can be defined as follows:

- `text, textarea`: The standard HTML elements
- `email`: The HTML5 input e-mail type
- `integer`: The HTML5 input number type (used by the HTML5 browsers)
- `password`: The standard HTML password field

- `money`: This allows you to specify currency and provide options to customize input and output of data

- `number`: This specializes in formatting numbers, allows to define precision, rounding, and so on

- `percent`: This specializes in handling percentage data

- `search`: The HTML5 input type search, supported by some browsers

- `url`: This prepends submitted value with `http://.` if the protocol is not defined

There are also built-in types for choices (selects, radio buttons, and so on) and date/time handling:

- `choice`: This renders the select/checkbox/radio button elements with given options

- `entity`: This is a special choice field, designed to load options from an entity

- `language`, `country`, `timezone`, `currency`: These allow the selection of language from a large list of languages, countries, time zones, or currencies

- `date`, `datetime`, `time`, `birthday`: The various fields useful for handling the date and time (rendered as grouped select boxes)

There are also other more advanced field types, collections, repeated fields, and file fields, and you can also use one of the form type object to embed it into another form, so you can easily define your own subset of fields.

Validation and form processing

So far, we have discussed the process of form creation. After we create the form, we usually need to validate the data provided, and we need to save the date somewhere. With Symfony2, these steps are pretty easy.

To make validation possible, we need to define rules for it. In Symfony2, we can define them in several ways. You can define constraints within the entity field (using annotations), within the form (as constraints option), and you can create validation YML configuration files. You should choose the way best for your own project clarity.

The easiest method is to provide validation within the form type, but again, it's not the best place to put constraints in (although it's useful if you are not using entities). If we work with entities, the best practice seems to be keeping the validation rules in the same place where we define the entity field.

Let's modify our entity class to support validation and make the name field required. Let's modify our entity in the `src/AppBundle/Entity/Task.php` file:

```php
<?php

namespace AppBundle\Entity;

use Doctrine\ORM\Mapping as ORM;
use Symfony\Component\Validator\Constraints as Assert;

/**
 * @ORM\Entity
 * @ORM\Table(name="todo_task")
 */
class Task
{
    /*...*/

    /**
     * @ORM\Column(type="string", length=255)
     * @Assert\NotBlank()
     */
        private $name;
    /* ... */
```

As you can see, we have added a new use statement for the constraints rules, and we have added a new `NotBlank` constraint rule to the entity. That's it. Now we can use this within the form, and if the data is valid, we can store our entity in the database.

Symfony2, by default, supports the following constraints:

- `NotBlank()`: This will make a value required
- `Blank()`: This will make sure that a value is empty or null
- `NotNull()`: This will make sure that a value is not equal to null
- `Null()`: This will make sure that a value is equal to null
- `True()` / `False()`: This will make sure that a value is true or false
- `Type()`: This will make sure that a value is of a specific data type
- `Email()`: This validates that a value is a valid e-mail
- `Length()`: This validates that a given string is between some minimum and maximum values
- `Url()`: This validates that a value is a valid URL

- `Regex()`: This validates that a value matches a regular expression
- `Ip()`: This validates that a value is a valid IP
- `Uuid()`: This validates that a value is a valid UUID
- `Range()`: This validates that a number is between some minimum and maximum number

There are also validators for files, images, comparison constraints, date constraints, collection constraints, and financial constraints. You can also define your own constraints very easily.

To process the form, we need to add the following code to our controller:

```
/* ... */
class TaskController extends Controller
{
    public function listAction(Request $request)
    {
        /* ... */
        $form = $this->createForm(new TaskType(), $newTask);

        $form->handleRequest($request);

        if ($form->isValid()) {
            $task = $form->getData();

            $em->persist($task);
            $em->flush();

            return $this->redirect($this->generateUrl('homepage'));
        }

        /* ... */
```

The newly added code executes the form validation, and if the data is valid, stores it in the database. After a successful save, it's a good practice to make a redirect to clear the data, as well as to protect the user from double-sending the data through the back button.

Now, when you add some data, your new entries should be visible within your table.

Theming form elements

So far our form does not look too pretty. It's just a basic form without any fancy styles. Symfony2 provides a very flexible way to customize form rendering using Twig templates called form theme.

Form theme is just a regular Twig template but filled with blocks to render form rows, labels, inputs, errors, text areas, select boxes, checkboxes, and so on.

By default, Symfony2 uses a theme called `form_div_layout.html.twig`. The file with this form style is located in `vendor/symfony/symfony/src/Symfony/Bridge/Twig/Resources/views/Form/form_div_layout.html.twig`, and it is good to review this and see how it's organized. It is, of course, possible to change this easily.

Let's create our own theme based on the default theme. Create the `app/Resources/views/Form/theme.html.twig` file and fill it with the following content:

```
{% use 'form_div_layout.html.twig' %}

{%- block form -%}
    {{- form_start(form, { attr: { class: 'ui form small', novalidate:
true }}) -}}
    {{- form_widget(form) -}}
    {{- form_end(form) -}}
{%- endblock form -%}

{%- block form_row %}
    <div class="field">
        {{ form_label(form) }}
        {{ form_errors(form) }}
        {{ form_widget(form) }}
    </div>
{% endblock form_row %}

{%- block date_widget -%}
    <div class="inline fields">
        <div class="field">
            {{- form_widget(form.year, { attr: { class: 'ui dropdown'
} }) -}}
        </div>
        <div class="field">
            {{- form_widget(form.month, { attr: { class: 'ui dropdown'
} }) -}}
        </div>
        <div class="field">
```

```
                {{- form_widget(form.day, { attr: { class: 'ui dropdown' }
}) -}}
        </div>
    </div>
{%- endblock date_widget -%}
```

The preceding code defines a few blocks and adds some classes to the `form` element, `field` element, and date widget.

In Symfony2, you can define multiple blocks to handle various form elements. For example, you can define `date_widget`. In our case, this is responsible for displaying three select boxes with date values, but you can also define `date_row` to organize label and error input.

After adding this file, we need to slightly modify our view where we placed the form:

```
{% extends '::base.html.twig' %}

{% form_theme form 'Form/theme.html.twig' %}

{% block body %}
    {# ... #}
    <p>New task:</p>
    <div style="width: 585px;">
        {{ form(form) }}
    </div>
{% endblock %}

{% block javascripts %}
    {{ parent() }}
    <script>
        $('.dropdown').dropdown();
    </script>
{% endblock %}
```

After refreshing, you will notice that the form looks much better than it did previously. To complete our work, we also need to provide styles for the submit element. We will modify the `TaskType` class as follows:

```
class TaskType extends AbstractType
{
    public function buildForm(FormBuilderInterface $builder, array
$options)
    {
        $builder
            ->add('name')
```

```
        ->add('notes')
        ->add('due_date')
        ->add('add', 'submit', [
            'label' => 'Add Task',
            'attr' => ['class' => 'ui primary button']
        ])
    ;
}
```

After we modify this file and refresh it, you should see a much better looking form. There are many ways to modify the form rendering capabilities. In addition to form themes, you can modify the field directly by using the form_row, form_widget, and form_errors functions, and you can apply the theme only to one of the form elements.

Transforming data

When we created our TaskType class, we skipped the tags property as this was not a simple text or date field. The tags property is related to the Tag table with the M:N relation, so we could present it as a list of checkboxes or a select box. However, people are used to fill tags with comma-separated values, so let's try to convert our objects to comma-separated tag names when displaying a field and convert them back when saving data to the database.

To present a list of objects (tags) as comma-separated values and to convert them back to tags, we need to create a data transformer. A data transformer is a class implementing DataTransformerInterface and allows us to transform our data to various formats. As an example—a data transformer is used when the date or date/time field type is used.

Create a src/AppBundle/Form/DataTransformer/TagDataTransformer.php file as follows:

```php
<?php

namespace AppBundle\Form\DataTransformer;

use AppBundle\Entity\Tag;
use Doctrine\ORM\EntityManager;
use Symfony\Component\Form\DataTransformerInterface;

class TagDataTransformer implements DataTransformerInterface
{
    /**
     * @var EntityManager
```

```
    */
    private $em;

    /**
     * @param EntityManager $em
     */
    public function __construct(EntityManager $em)
    {
        $this->em = $em;
    }

    /**
     * Transforms an objects (Tags) to a string.
     */
    public function transform($tags)
    {
        if (null === $tags) {
            return "";
        }

        $output = [];

        foreach ($tags as $tag) {
            $output[] = $tag->getName();
        }

        return join(', ', $output);
    }

    /**
     * Transforms a string to a tag.
     */
    public function reverseTransform($tags)
    {
        if (!$tags) {
            return [];
        }

        $output = [];
        $tagsArray = explode(',', $tags);

        foreach ($tagsArray as $name) {
            $name = trim($name);
```

```
        $tag = $this->em
            ->getRepository('AppBundle:Tag')
            ->findOneBy(array('name' => $name))
        ;

        if (!$tag) {
            $tag = new Tag();
            $tag->setName($name);
            $this->em->persist($tag);
        }

        $output[] = $tag;
    }

    return $output;
    }
}
```

The preceding code transforms a list of tags into comma-separated values. This was the easy part. When reversing, however, we need to verify whether the specific tag exists in the database, and if not, we need to create them, and return a list of tags to be attached to our Task object.

To use the data transformer, we need to modify our TaskType form class and the buildForm method, as follows:

```php
<?php

namespace AppBundle\Form\Type;

use AppBundle\Form\DataTransformer\TagDataTransformer;
use Symfony\Component\Form\AbstractType;
use Symfony\Component\Form\FormBuilderInterface;
use Symfony\Component\OptionsResolver\OptionsResolver;

class TaskType extends AbstractType
{
    public function buildForm(FormBuilderInterface $builder, array $options)
    {
        $em = $options['em'];
        $trans = new TagDataTransformer($em);

        $builder
            ->add('name')
```

```
            ->add('notes')
            ->add('due_date')
            ->add(
                $builder
                    ->create('tags', 'text')
                    ->addModelTransformer($trans)
            )
            ->add('add', 'submit', [
                'label' => 'Add Task',
                'attr' => ['class' => 'ui primary button'
            ]])
        ;
    }

    public function configureOptions(OptionsResolver $resolver)
    {
        $resolver
            ->setDefaults([
                'data_class' => 'AppBundle\Entity\Task',
            ])
            ->setRequired(['em'])
            ->setAllowedTypes('em', 'Doctrine\ORM\EntityManager')
        ;
    }

    public function getName()
    {
        return 'task';
    }
}
```

The preceding code applies the data transformer, requires an extra option from the form type, and enforces data type on that form option. Note that we have applied the data transformer to the tags property of the entity, and we have manually defined the field as text.

To complete everything, we need to update our form class in `TaskController`. Change the following line:

```
$form = $this->createForm(new TaskType(), $newTask);
```

This has to be changed to:

```
$form = $this->createForm(new TaskType(), $newTask, ['em' => $em]);
```

Now try to add the new data. After submitting the form, you should see the data with the attached tags.

You can also create data transformers as service, and define your own form data type (text, number, and so on) with an attached data transformer (just as it happens with the `date` or `datetime` type).

Summary

In this chapter, we have learned a lot about form creation, validation, and visual rendering. Although it may seem very hard at the beginning to start with this class, it is a very flexible and powerful tool and allows the creation of very complex form structures.

In the next chapter, we will learn about Symfony2 security, creating a user entity, and handling login process.

5
Security and Handling Users

After sorting out basic views and form creation, we need to have a way to identify users and to display only their customized tasks. For this task to take place, we need to implement a basic authentication process and bind our to-do tasks to the users. Also, we need to enforce our authentication and prevent anonymous actions. We need to do this because all tasks need an owner and a person responsible for them. We do not want to share our own tasks list with others.

In this chapter, we will cover the following topics:

* Review Symfony2 built-in security capabilities
* Install a user manager bundle to make user handling easier
* User registration

Security handling

Symfony2 handles all the security-related actions through its own security system. This system is very flexible and powerful, but requires some setup. We need to start our journey through this system by reviewing its initial configuration file located in the `app/config/security.yml` file. Here, we still see some references after the demo app, which we will sort out in this chapter.

Let's review this:

```
# To get started with security, check out the documentation:
# http://symfony.com/doc/current/book/security.html
security:

    providers:
        in_memory:
            memory: ~
```

```
firewalls:
    # disables authentication for assets and the
    # profiler, adapt it according to your needs
    dev:
        pattern: ^/(_(profiler|wdt)|css|images|js)/
        security: false

    main:
        anonymous: ~
        # activate different ways to authenticate

        # http_basic: ~


        # form_login: ~
```

The preceding file contains only few basic sections. Usually, this file is split into four main sections. The first section, called as encoders, defines what kind of encoding is used for the password. This can be plain text, various SHA-encodings, as well as bcrypt, and so on. In the preceding example, we have a plain text encryption.

The second section defines role hierarchy. You can define any role you want in any hierarchy you need. This system is very flexible, and allows you to inherit permissions when your role increases, and also allows you to entirely keep separate roles and their permissions.

The firewall section is one of the most interesting. It allows you to define the paths protected by specific rules, choose various authentication methods (that is, http basic-auth or through form login), and define various related options. This section is the most crucial part when it comes to securing various parts of your application.

> It is worth going to the official Symfony2 SecurityBundleConfiguration section at http://symfony.com/doc/current/reference/configuration/security.html to review all the available sections and their options.

The last section commonly configured is the access control section. In this section, you can secure your specific URL pattern. This list can be detailed, so you can, for example, protect /panel with one rule and /panel/login with another. Just remember that Symfony2 stops at the first matching rule and doesn't look further. In this area, you can also limit access by other conditions, such as IP address.

The `security.yml` file is not the only place where you can limit access to a specific resource. You can still do this within the controller and/or within the twig template, if you need to limit access based on some more sophisticated logic. But, generally, the `security.yml` file is your starting point.

Installing the user manager bundle

While Symfony2 has some basic user handling, there is a very popular bundle, `FOSUserBundle`, created by the Friends of Symfony group. In the first chapter, we added this bundle to the composer, but now, we need to properly install and configure it.

First, we need to add the bundle to `app/AppKernel.php` as follows:

```
/* ... */
new AppBundle\AppBundle(),
new FOS\UserBundle\FOSUserBundle(),
);
```

We need to add configuration to this. You can directly add this to your `app/config/config.yml` file or create a separate file for this and import the resource. Creating a separate file makes it easier to manage, and sometimes to copy to other projects.

Let's create the `app/config/fos/user.yml` file with the following content:

```
fos_user:
    db_driver: orm
    firewall_name: main
    user_class: AppBundle\Entity\User
```

Add this to the `config.yml` file in the imports section. Also, since this bundle is using translations, we need to enable it by uncommenting the translator field as follows:

```
imports:
    - { resource: parameters.yml }
    - { resource: security.yml }
    - { resource: services.yml }
    - { resource: fos/user.yml }

framework:
  #esi:            ~
  translator:       { fallbacks: ["%locale%"] }
```

This will tell the manager which database driver and firewall we are using and what the name of the user class is. Now, we need to modify our security rules. Enter the security.yml file again and change it as follows:

```
# you can read more about security in the related section of the
documentation
# http://symfony.com/doc/current/book/security.html
security:
    encoders:
        FOS\UserBundle\Model\UserInterface: bcrypt


role_hierarchy:
        ROLE_ADMIN:        ROLE_USER
        ROLE_SUPER_ADMIN: [ROLE_USER, ROLE_ADMIN, ROLE_ALLOWED_TO_
SWITCH]


providers:
    fos_userbundle:
        id: fos_user.user_provider.username_email


# the main part of the security, where you can set
# up firewalls for specific sections of your app
firewalls:
    # disables authentication for assets and the
    # profiler, adapt it according to your needs
    dev:
        pattern:  ^/(_(profiler|wdt)|css|images|js)/
        security: false
    main:
        pattern: ^/
        form_login:
            provider: fos_userbundle
            csrf_provider: form.csrf_provider
            use_forward: false
            login_path: /login
            check_path: /login_check
        logout:
            path: /logout
        anonymous:      true


# with these settings you can restrict or allow access
# for different parts of your application based on roles,
# ip, host or methods
#
```

```
access_control:
    - { path: ^/login$, role: IS_AUTHENTICATED_ANONYMOUSLY }
    - { path: ^/logout$, role: IS_AUTHENTICATED_ANONYMOUSLY }
    - { path: ^/login-check$, role: IS_AUTHENTICATED_ANONYMOUSLY }
    - { path: ^/.*, role: ROLE_USER }
```

We modified practically every section in the preceding code, except the roles hierarchy, which was fine for our needs, so we configured the encoder to `bcrypt` (one of the algorithms that is now considered as the most secure). Also, we set the encoder to the one based on the FOS model interface.

In the providers section, we defined the FOS provider and removed the in-memory provider. In Symfony2, you can have multiple providers—each firewall that is defined can use a different provider. Next is the firewall section. Here, we defined the main firewall and removed the demo firewalls. Note the `form_login` section within the firewall. Here, we have defined the FOS provider and provided paths for login, check path, and logout. Note that here we have selected a provider too. Also note that the order of elements within the firewall is important, especially if one of them is used across the whole site (this should be placed last).

In the last section, we have defined a few anonymous paths and requested that all other paths should require users with the ROLE_USER role.

Now we need to define a new entity to store the user details. The FOS bundle comes with the entity prepared and packed as an abstract entity, which means that we can inherit all of its properties and fields, just like for a normal object, and this will be used to generate a normal SQL table.

Create the entity in the `src/AppBundle/Entity/User.php` file as follows:

```php
<?php

namespace AppBundle\Entity;

use FOS\UserBundle\Entity\User as BaseUser;

use Doctrine\ORM\Mapping as ORM;

/**
 * @ORM\Entity
 * @ORM\Table(name="todo_user")
 */
class User extends BaseUser
{
    /**
```

```
 * @ORM\Id
 * @ORM\Column(type="integer")
 * @ORM\GeneratedValue(strategy="AUTO")
 */
protected $id;
}
```

As you can see, this class is very simple and extends all the required fields from the base class. Now, we need to generate the required getters/setters as follows:

```
php app/console doctrine:generate:entities --no-backup AppBundle
php app/console doctrine:schema:update --force
```

We need to add routing for the login and logout operations. Open the `app/config/routing.yml` file and add the following:

```
fos_user_security:
    resource: "@FOSUserBundle/Resources/config/routing/security.xml"
    prefix: /
```

This fragment will import the routings responsible for the login and logout actions. Now we can fire up our server and verify whether we can see the login screen.

The login screen is very basic, not styled. To style it, we need to implement our own styling. One of the main Symfony2 features is the very flexible overwrite system. If we want to overwrite any of the bundles templates, we can do this by placing the template file in the specific directory in `app/Resources`.

In our case, as we want to override the `FOSUserBundle` view, we need to create the `app/Resources/FOSUserBundle/views/Security/login.html.twig` file. Why this name? If you look into the `vendors/` structure and look for our user bundle, you will notice that it has the `Resources/views` directory containing a few files. You can override every one of them by placing it in the `app/Resources` structure and using the registered bundle name (in this case, `FOSUserBundle`).

Open the newly created file, and add the following content:

```
{% extends "::base.html.twig" %}

{% trans_default_domain 'FOSUserBundle' %}

{% block body %}
<div class="ui one column stackable center aligned page grid"
style="margin-top: 150px;">
    <div class="column twelve wide">
    {% if error %}
```

```
            <div class="ui error message">
                {{ error|trans({}, 'FOSUserBundle') }}
            </div>
        {% endif %}

        <form action="{{ path("fos_user_security_check") }}" method="post"
class="ui form">
            <input type="hidden" name="_csrf_token" value="{{ csrf_token
}}" />

            <div class="inline field">
                <label for="username">{{ 'security.login.username'|trans
}}</label>
                <div class="ui icon input">
                    <input type="text" id="username" name="_username"
value="{{ last_username }}" required="required" />
                    <i class="user icon"></i>
                </div>
            </div>

            <div class="inline field">
                <label for="password">{{ 'security.login.password'|trans
}}</label>
                <div class="ui icon input">
                    <input type="password" id="password" name="_password"
required="required" />
                    <i class="lock icon"></i>
                </div>
            </div>

            <input class="ui button" type="submit" id="_submit" name="_
submit" value="{{ 'security.login.submit'|trans }}" />
        </form>
        </div>
    </div>
{% endblock body %}
```

Now we can refresh the site, and see the styled login form. You can note that there are some tags used for translation. We will deal with this in the next chapter.

Now, since we have a working login screen, we need to amend our `Task` entity to support the users, list view, and form creation to support the logged in users.

First, we need to modify our `Task` entity as follows:

```
// ...
/**
 * @ORM\Column(type="boolean")
 */
private $finished = 0;

// add the following code
/**
 * @ORM\ManyToOne(targetEntity="User")
 */
private $user;
```

This extends our `Task` table and relates it to the newly created `User` table.

After this, we need to update our database and generate the getters/setters as follows:

```
php app/console doctrine:schema:update --force
php app/console doctrine:generate:entities --no-backup AppBundle
```

Then, we need to update our fixtures by adding a new file as follows:

```php
<?php

namespace AppBundle\DataFixtures\ORM;

use Doctrine\Common\DataFixtures\AbstractFixture;
use Doctrine\Common\DataFixtures\OrderedFixtureInterface;
use Doctrine\Common\Persistence\ObjectManager;
use Symfony\Component\DependencyInjection\ContainerAwareInterface;
use Symfony\Component\DependencyInjection\ContainerInterface;

class LoadUserData extends AbstractFixture implements
OrderedFixtureInterface, ContainerAwareInterface
{
    /**
     * @var ContainerInterface
     */
    private $container;

    /**
     * {@inheritDoc}
     */
    public function setContainer(ContainerInterface $container = null)
```

```
    {
        $this->container = $container;
    }

    public function load(ObjectManager $manager)
    {
        $um = $this->container->get('fos_user.user_manager');

        $obj = $um->createUser();
        $obj->setUsername('todo');
        $obj->setEmail('todo@example.com');
        $obj->setPlainPassword('test');
        $obj->setRoles(['ROLE_USER']);
        $obj->setEnabled(true);

        $um->updateUser($obj);
        $this->addReference('user:'.$obj->getUsername(), $obj);
    }

    public function getOrder()
    {
        return 1;
    }
}
```

This file will load a to-do example user with the todo@example.com email and the test password. The user will have an attached ROLE_USER and will be enabled. Note that we have used a new interface called ContainerAwareInterface, and loaded the container to the fixtures class. This way, we can use any service available within the container at the time of running the command. We loaded the user manager service, which handles operations such as hashing passwords and saving the user data.

Now we need to add an user to our example task by modifying src/AppBundle/DataFixtures/ORM/LoadTaskData.php and adding the following:

```
$obj->setUser($this->getReference('user:todo'));
```

The preceding code has to be added before this:

```
$manager->persist($obj);
```

We can now reload the data as follows:

```
$ php app/console doctrine:fixtures:load
```

Now, there is one final thing that we need to update. In our task controller, we need to filter tasks by users, and we need to add a user to the newly created task. Modify the file as follows:

```
// ...
public function listAction(Request $request)
{
    $this->denyAccessUnlessGranted('ROLE_USER');

    $em = $this->getDoctrine()->getManager();

    $tasks = $em->getRepository('AppBundle:Task')
        ->createQueryBuilder('t')
        ->where('t.finished = :finished')
        ->andWhere('t.user = :user')
        ->orderBy('t.due_date', 'ASC')
        ->setParameter('finished', false)
        ->setParameter('user', $this->getUser())
        ->getQuery()
        ->getResult();

    // ...

    if ($form->isValid()) {
        $task = $form->getData();
        $task->setUser($this->getUser());
```

The first line here with denyAccessUnlessGranted isn't really necessary because we have limited our access within the security file. However, sometimes it is required to verify permissions with more sophisticated methods; then, this method comes in handy. It can also take an object as a second parameter, so you can verify the access permissions not just for the whole action, but also for a single object.

We also added the getUser() helper method to our filter criteria and to our newly created task to load the user object from the security handler. The user object loaded here will be our user entity.

Now, you can log in to your application and add/view tasks related to your logged in user. To polish our application more, we will add the logout feature to our base template in the app/Resources/views/base.html.twig file, right after the body tag as follows:

```
<body>
        {% if is_granted('ROLE_USER') %}
```

```
<div class="ui menu">
    <div class="item right">
        Logged in as: <strong>{{ app.user.username }}</strong>
| <a href="{{ path('fos_user_security_logout') }}">Log-out</a>
    </div>
</div>
{% endif %}
```

The interesting part—Twig exposes the user object to the app variable (the same entity as controller). Also, there is a quick helper method to verify the user role and permissions—`is_granted`.

Together, these methods are the most popular ways of handling user permissions. Sometimes it is handy to write some more complex rules. Symfony2 offers few more advanced mechanisms to deal with advanced concepts. You can use **Access Control List (ACL)**, which is a very complicated piece and often criticized for this. There is also an alternative, you can write in the so-called voter.

Both ways allow you to define more complex rules, and even relate your security to a single database object.

User registration

Now we can quickly add a way to register users. This is already built in FOS; we just need to use it. To do so, we need to (as with login) enable routing, add a template, and link to the registration form. Add the following rule to routing:

```
fos_user_registration:
  resource: "@FOSUserBundle/Resources/config/routing/registration.xml"
  prefix: /register
```

Update the security file with a new access control entry at the start as follows:

```
access_control:
    - { path: ^/register, role: IS_AUTHENTICATED_ANONYMOUSLY }
```

This modification will add the required routings. Now we need to override the template for registration. To do this, add two files. One file is `app/Resources/FOSUserBundle/views/Registration/register.html.twig` with the following content:

```
{% extends "::base.html.twig" %}

{% trans_default_domain 'FOSUserBundle' %}
```

```
{% block body %}
<div class="ui one column stackable page grid" style="margin-top:
150px;">
    <div class="column twelve wide">
        <form action="{{ path('fos_user_registration_register') }}" {{
form_enctype(form) }} method="POST" class="ui form">
            {{ form_widget(form) }}
            <div style="margin-top: 20px;">
                <input class="ui button" type="submit" value="{{
'registration.submit'|trans }}" />
            </div>
        </form>
    </div>
</div>
{% endblock body %}
```

This will add the view for the registration form. The other file with the confirmation message is at the `app/Resources/FOSUserBundle/views/Registration/confirmed.html.twig` location with the following code:

```
{% extends "::base.html.twig" %}

{% trans_default_domain 'FOSUserBundle' %}

{% block body %}
<div class="ui one column stackable page grid" style="margin-top:
150px;">
    <div class="column twelve wide">
        <p>{{ 'registration.confirmed'|trans({'%username%': user.
username}) }}</p>
        <p><a href="{{ path('homepage') }}">Back to homepage</a></p>
    </div>
</div>
{% endblock body %}
```

This modification will add everything, and our registration will be available under the `/register` link. To make this visible to the users, we need to link it, so again modify the `app/Resources/views/base.html.twig` file in the menu section that we added just after the body with the new code, as follows:

```
<body>
    <div class="ui menu">
        <div class="item right">
            {% if is_granted('ROLE_USER') %}
```

```
                    Logged in as: <strong>{{ app.user.username }}</
strong> | <a href="{{ path('fos_user_security_logout') }}">Log-out</a>
                {% else %}
                    <a href="{{ path('fos_user_registration_register')
}}">Register</a>
                {% endif %}
            </div>
        </div>
```

Now we have a fully implemented login, logout, and registration functionality.

Summary

In this chapter, we have learned about the Symfony security system and explored the way to log in to it, how to register a user, and how to add a user to the database through fixtures.

In the next chapter, we will focus on translations, the way to provide interface translations, and we will discuss the various strategies for database translations.

6
Translation

One of the most common requirements when building a new site is to have the ability to present it in another language. The translation process can be very difficult. We need to consider various aspects of translating a website—starting from interface translation, choosing default culture, formatting numbers, currencies, and dates to localized ones, and finally, allowing the user to put content in multiple languages.

In this chapter, we will focus on the following:

- Reviewing various translation formats available in Symfony2
- Creating translation files
- How to use translations in all areas of application
- How to choose the right translation strategy

Translations

Symfony2 provides some basic mechanism to make translations easier. In our application, we enabled translations in the previous chapter as `FOSUserBundle` was using this feature to present its interface.

As a reminder, to enable translation we need to uncomment it in the `config.yml` file:

```
framework:
    #esi:               ~
    translator:         { fallbacks: ["%locale%"] }
```

Using translations in a controller

Translator in Symfony2 is a service, just like almost anything else. It means you can use it in any controller, and you can inject it into your own services. You can also access it in Twig, as it was presented in the previous chapter.

The translation service exposes a method called `trans`. As an example, to use it in a controller we need to call the translation service:

```
$this->get('translator')->trans('Hello user');
```

The `trans` method can accept four parameters as follows:

```
trans(id, parameters, domain, locale)
```

The first parameter is the string to be translated. The second parameter is an array to be used as a list of parameters. The third string is called translation domain. We will describe this further in this chapter. The last is the locale. User locale is taken automatically, and when it does not exist, the fallback locale is used.

Let's look at the following example taken from our login page:

```
{% extends "::base.html.twig" %}

{% trans_default_domain 'FOSUserBundle' %}

{% block body %}
{# ... #}

    <form action="{{ path("fos_user_security_check") }}" method="post"
class="ui form">
        <input type="hidden" name="_csrf_token" value="{{ csrf_token
}}" />

        <div class="inline field">
            <label for="username">{{ 'security.login.username'|trans
}}</label>
{# ... #}
```

In the preceding example, we are using the `twig` filter for internationalization. Note that we have changed the translation domain to `FOSUserBundle`. By default, translation domain is set to messages. What does this means? The translator is looking for specific translations in files with the `domain.locale.format`, for example, `messages.en.yml`. Translations can be located in the bundle resources directory, that is, `src/AppBundle/Resources/translations/`, or they can be added to the `app/Resources/translations/` global resources directory.

Usually when you are installing a bundle with translation support, authors are using bundle name as a domain name. Also, it is possible to override vendor translations by overriding their catalogue files with your own in the app/Resources directory. For example, to override the FOSUserBundle translations for English language, we need to create the app/Resources/translations/FOSUserBundle.en.yml file and provide our own translations there. The following code is an example:

```
# Security
security:
    login:
        username: "Your Username:"
        password: "Your Password:"
```

Changes label in form, from Username to Your Username, and from Password to Your Password.

Translation file formats

The Symfony2 translator components support a wide range of formats: CSV, INI, YML, PHP, gettext, JSON, and XLIFF. You can choose either one of these. In practice, the most commonly used formats are YML and XLIFF. The first one is much more simple and easy to edit, while the second one is supported by tools used by professional translators.

An example of YML format (part of the FOSUserBundle translation) is as follows:

```
security:
    login:
        username: "Username:"
        password: "Password:"
        remember_me: Remember me
        submit: Login
```

The same translation using PHP is as follows:

```
return array(
    'security.login.username' => 'Username:',
    'security.login.password' => 'Password:',
    'security.login.remember_me' => 'Remember me:',
    'security.login.submit' => 'Login:',
);
```

Now with the XLIFF format:

```
<?xml version="1.0"?>
<xliff version="1.2" xmlns="urn:oasis:names:tc:xliff:document:1.2">
```

```
        <file source-language="en" datatype="plaintext" original="file.
ext">
            <body>
                <trans-unit id="1">
                    <source>security.login.username</source>
                    <target>Username:</target>
                </trans-unit>
                <trans-unit id="2">
                    <source>security.login.password</source>
                    <target>Password:</target>
                </trans-unit>
                <trans-unit id="3">
                    <source>security.login.remember_me</source>
                    <target>Remember me:</target>
                </trans-unit>
                <trans-unit id="4">
                    <source>security.login.submit</source>
                    <target>Login:</target>
                </trans-unit>
            </body>
        </file>
    </xliff>
```

While XLIFF file seems to be most complicated, it is again worth noting that it is supported by a lot of various tools, especially the ones for translators. Also since Symfony 2.6, it has been possible to pass notes to translators and define context (which is sometimes very important):

```
<trans-unit id="1">
  <source>security.login.username</source>
    <target>Username:</target>
    <note from="Wojciech">
      This is displayed as label near to login input text.
      Translation should not have more than 20 characters.
    </note>
</trans-unit>
```

Since Symfony 2.6, it has been also possible to turn on logs to indicate strings with missing translations. To do so, you can alter your `config.yml` file as follows:

```
framework:
    #esi:              ~
    translator:        { fallback: %locale%, logging: true }
```

When logging is enabled, Symfony2 will add the missing translation to the log file of the current environment (development or production). The default value is set to `%kernel.debug%` (it will be true in development mode and false in production).

Variables and pluralization

It is worth discussing situations where you have variables within your translation string, for example, when you have a shopping basket and you want to present translations for all the cases:

- No products in the basket
- One product in the basket
- More than one product in the basket

Let's handle the last case first. To support variables, we would create a translation (YML) like this:

```
basket:
    products: You have %number% products in basket
```

Now when using this key, we can provide the number of products as a variable. To do so, we can provide the variable to be replaced as the second parameter in the `trans` function or filter, for example (within any controller), consider the following:

```
$translator = $this->get('translator');
$message = $translator
    ->trans('basket.products', ['%number%' => 5]);
```

This will result in the string, `You have 5 products in basket`.

Pluralization, however, is a more complex situation. In many languages, there can be many plural forms and handling them may vary. To handle pluralization, we have another `transChoice` method. This method accepts a special form of translated messages and the number of objects as argument. Given our previous example, we could write the following:

```
basket:
    products: '{0} You have no products in basket|{1} You have one
product in basket|[2,Inf[ You have %number% products in basket.'
```

Now, we can use it in the translator like this:

```
$message = $translator
    ->transChoice('basket.products', 5, ['%number%' => 5]);
```

This will result in the following message:

```
You have 10 products in basket.
```

Have a look at the following translator:

```
$message = $translator
  ->transChoice('basket.products', 1, ['%number%' => 1]);
```

This will give you the following output:

```
You have one product in basket
```

The translation strategy

While creating translation keys, you can take two approaches. The first approach is to create a key based on natural language. So, for example, you would write in Twig as follows:

```
<p>{{ 'Hello World'|trans }}<p>
```

While this approach is convenient during development, it may cause a lot of issues later, especially when you want to replace such a string with another one. To avoid such situations, the preferred way of creating translations is to provide translation keys. Apart from fixing the preceding issue, keys also have a few more advantages as follows:

- You can organize them in groups when using YML format
- It is easier to detect missing translation, without analyzing log files
- They are usually shorter and easier to manage

It is, of course, entirely up to you what you will use.

Using translation keys

In our ToDo application, we will use translation keys. It is handy to rewrite the form template to automatically create keys for labels. Insert the following code in `Resources/views/Form/theme.html.twig`:

```
{% block form_label %}
    {% spaceless %}
        {% if label is empty %}
            {% set label = "label." ~ form.vars.name %}
        {% endif %}
        {{ parent() }}
```

```
    {% endspaceless %}
  {% endblock form_label %}
```

Now, we need to make a few replacements in our files. In the `src/AppBundle/Form/Type/TaskType.php` file, make the following replacements:

Original code	New code

<pre>->add('add', 'submit', [
  'label' => 'Add Task',
  'attr' => [
    'class' =>
    'ui primary button'
]])</pre>
	<pre>->add('add', 'submit', [
	  'label' =>
	    'label.add_task',
	  'attr' => [
	    'class' =>
	    'ui primary button'
	]])</pre>

In the `Resources/views/base.html.twig` file, make the following replacements:

Original code	New code

<pre><div class="ui menu">
  <div class="item right">
    {% if is_
granted('ROLE_USER') %}
      Logged in as:
<strong>{{ app.user.username
}}</strong> | <a href="{{
path('fos_user_security_
logout') }}">Log-out</a>
    {% else %}
      <a href="{{
path('fos_user_registration_
register') }}">Register</a>
    {% endif %}
  </div>
</div></pre>
	<pre><div class="ui menu">
	  <div class="item right">
	    {% if is_
	granted('ROLE_USER') %}
	      {{ 'top_
	menu.logged_in'|trans({
	'%username%': app.user.
	username })|raw }} | <a
	href="{{ path('fos_user_
	security_logout') }}">{{
	'top_menu.logout'|trans }}</
	a>
	    {% else %}
	      <a href="{{
	path('fos_user_registration_
	register') }}">{{ 'top_menu.
	register'|trans }}</a>
	    {% endif %}
	  </div>
	</div></pre>

In the `Resources/views/task/list.html.twig` file, make the following replacements:

Original code	New code
`<h2 class="ui aligned header">Your tasks list</h2>` `<p class="ui aligned">Below you will find your unfinished tasks</p>`	`<h2 class="ui aligned header">{{ 'todo_list.title'|trans }}</h2>` `    <p class="ui aligned">{{ 'todo_list.description'|trans }}</p>`

`<tr>`
 `  <th>Name</th>`
 `  <th>Notes</th>`
 `  <th>Tags</th>`
 `  <th>Due</th>`
 `</tr>`
	`<tr>`
	 `  <th>{{ 'todo_list.name'|trans }}</th>`
	 `  <th>{{ 'todo_list.notes'|trans }}</th>`
	 `  <th>{{ 'todo_list.tags'|trans }}</th>`
	 `  <th>{{ 'todo_list.due'|trans }}</th>`
	 `</tr>`

`<tr>`
 `  <td colspan="4" class="center aligned">`
 `    <h2>There are no unfinished tasks at the moment. Good Job!</h2>`
 `  </td>`
 `</tr>`
	`<tr>`
	 `  <td colspan="4" class="center aligned">`
	 `    <h2>{{ 'todo_list.no_unfinished'|trans }}</h2>`
	 `  </td>`
	 `</tr>`

`<p>New task:</p>`	`<p>{{ 'todo_list.new'|trans }}</p>`

In all these changes, we replaced the original text with new translation keys. Now we need to create a translation file. To make this easier, Symfony2 provides a method to extract translations from templates. Let's call this:

```
php app/console translation:update --output-format=yml --dump-messages
--force en
```

You should now see your translations in the `app/Resources/translations/messages.en.yml` file, with the following content:

```
top_menu.logged_in: __top_menu.logged_in
top_menu.logout: __top_menu.logout
```

```
top_menu.register: __top_menu.register
todo_list.title: __todo_list.title
todo_list.description: __todo_list.description
todo_list.name: __todo_list.name
todo_list.notes: __todo_list.notes
todo_list.tags: __todo_list.tags
todo_list.due: __todo_list.due
todo_list.no_unfinished: __todo_list.no_unfinished
todo_list.new: __todo_list.new
```

Let's replace this and organize, as shown in the following code:

```
top_menu:
    logged_in: Logged in as: <strong>%username%</strong>
    logout: Log-out
    register: Register

todo_list:
    title: Your tasks list
    description: Below you will find your unfinished tasks
    name: Name
    notes: Notes
    tags: Tags
    due: Due
    no_unfinished: There are no unfinished tasks at the moment. Good
Job!
    new: New task
```

Clear the cache (sometime translations can refresh only after you clear the cache), and then you can refresh the site. Most of the elements should now be translated, but you will notice that the form elements are not. They were not extracted automatically, because the name for the translation is created dynamically. To fix this, we will add this part manually. Add the following code to the translation file (at the end):

```
label:
    name: Name
    notes: Notes
    due_date: Due date
    tags: Tags
    add_task: Add task
```

We have completed our goal in this chapter. Now, based on this we can produce the file in different languages, but how to switch to it? There are two methods. You can set your locale based on routing or based on session. The routing method is recommended when you want all your language versions to be indexable. The session-based locale is handy, for example, if you store user preference in the database.

To allow the choice of locale in your routing, modify it to the following form:

```
homepage:
    path:       /{_locale}
    defaults: { _controller: AppBundle:Task:list, _locale: 'en' }
```

We have added a special parameter called {_locale}, which is used by Symfony2 to switch the locale. If the locale in the given language does not exist, the default (fallback) one will be used. To fully support this, we also need to add this to our security panel and the FOS routing. Modify app/config/routing.yml as follows:

```
# bundles routings
fos_user_security:
    resource: "@FOSUserBundle/Resources/config/routing/security.xml"
    prefix: /{_locale}

fos_user_registration:
    resource: "@FOSUserBundle/Resources/config/routing/registration.
xml"
    prefix: /{_locale}/register
```

Modify the security.yml file (the firewall section and paths) as follows:

```
        main:
            pattern: ^/
            form_login:
                provider: fos_userbundle
                csrf_provider: form.csrf_provider
                use_forward: false
                login_path: fos_user_security_login
                check_path: fos_user_security_check
            logout:
                path: fos_user_security_logout
            anonymous:      true


    # with these settings you can restrict or allow access for
different parts
    # of your application based on roles, ip, host or methods
    # http://symfony.com/doc/current/cookbook/security/access_control.
html
    access_control:
      - { path: ^/[a-z]+/register, role: IS_AUTHENTICATED_ANONYMOUSLY
}
      - { path: ^/[a-z]+/login$, role: IS_AUTHENTICATED_ANONYMOUSLY }
      - { path: ^/[a-z]+/logout$, role: IS_AUTHENTICATED_ANONYMOUSLY }
```

```
        - { path: ^/[a-z]+/login-check$, role: IS_AUTHENTICATED_
ANONYMOUSLY }
        - { path: ^/.*, role: ROLE_USER }
```

So what have we changed? We have changed our login/logout paths to be accessible under locale, and we have allowed the locale settings before the login/logout paths in the access control section.

Now, when you refresh with the default English locale, you should be redirected to /en/login rather than /login.

Database translations

Sometimes it is also required to translate database entries. Symfony2 does not solve this problem, however there are bundles to help you with this task.

Generally, there are three approaches to solve this problem. The first approach is to simply add the locale field to the entity. There are no bundles to help with this, and generally, this approach is good only in a few rare cases (as every entry in the database needs to be duplicated), but it's the simplest one to implement.

The second approach is to generate a special table and create translation entries here based on the entity name. It is implemented as a doctrine extension and available as a bundle called StofDoctrineExtensionsBundle. Among other useful extensions, it provides extensions for the Tree algorithm, allows the creation of Sluggable, Timestampable, Loggable, Sortable objects, and many more.

The third approach is called the indexBy approach, where there are subtables and subentities created to handle the translations of specific fields. This approach is used by three projects: A2lixI18nDoctrineBundle, KnpDoctrineExtension, and PrezentDoctrineTranslatableBundle.

Not all of them are actively developed, so you need to review them before making a decision about the Symfony2 version you are going to use and your requirements. Note that most of the actively developed projects require PHP 5.4 or higher versions.

There is also a bundle called A2LiXTranslationFormBundle to help you with rendering translation forms or the language switcher. It works with the previously mentioned bundles.

Summary

In this chapter, we discussed various translation options, and we've created translation files within our project. In the next chapter, we will add Ajax features to allow tasks to be finished, deleted and to be edited.

AJAX

In the current chapter, we will look at some of the tools designed to help us in developing REST APIs. We will use these tools to write missing functionality in our application. At the end of this chapter, we will be able to do the following:

- Edit an existing task
- Mark a task as finished
- Delete a task from the database

Symfony2 is a typical server-side PHP framework, so it does not offer a lot of built-in features to make frontend development easier. Typical issues that you may encounter are as follows:

- Handling translations and routings within JavaScript files
- Easily creating various non-standard HTTP requests such as PUT, PATCH, or DELETE
- Handling multiple response formats (for example, JSON/XML)
- Creating good API documentation
- Testing/verifying API calls and responses

The AJAX calls and, generally, raw API calls are nowadays one of the most popular functionalities you may encounter while developing a web application. Often, you will encounter requirements to support mobile applications or modern JavaScript frameworks such as AngularJS. Of course, we can (somehow) handle everything from the preceding list with a pure Symfony2, but thanks to framework extensibility and open source community, now we have a few great tools to improve our work.

Let's start traditionally with bundle installations and configurations. The bundles recommended for this chapter are as follows:

- `NelmioApiDocBundle`
- `FOSRestBundle`
- `JMSSerializerBundle`
- `FOSJSRoutingBundle`

We will describe the role of each of them while developing specific parts of code.

Installing and configuring REST features

First, we will need to install our bundles by typing the following:

```
$ composer require jms/serializer-bundle
$ composer require friendsofsymfony/rest-bundle
$ composer require friendsofsymfony/jsrouting-bundle
$ composer require nelmio/api-doc-bundle
```

Then, we need to modify the `AppKernel.php` file, and add our new bundles as follows:

```
// other bundles
new JMS\SerializerBundle\JMSSerializerBundle(),
new FOS\RestBundle\FOSRestBundle(),
new FOS\JsRoutingBundle\FOSJsRoutingBundle(),
new Nelmio\ApiDocBundle\NelmioApiDocBundle(),
);
```

This will activate the bundles. Some of them require a little additional configuration steps.

FOSRestBundle

We will start our configuration with `FOSRestBundle`. This bundle is used to automate request and response handling. It allows you to create routings based just on your action name. Also, the bundle guesses what kind of request you may need (POST, PUT, DELETE, or other), and tries to define the optimal routing compatible with the REST API principles. One of the great advantages of this bundle is that it works with various serializers, so it can handle not just simple arrays, but also whole objects and collection of objects. Internally, this bundle uses (and requires) a serializer to be installed.

We will not use a serializer in this chapter. We have installed
`JMSSerializerBundle` because `FOSRestBundle` requires at least one
serializer, but we will not be using it in the book. It is, however, worth
looking at the documentation to see what this library is capable of.

To start with the bundle, we need to add some minimal options that have to be
configured. As with the user, we will create a new file in `app/config/fos/rest.yml`
with the following content:

```
fos_rest:
    routing_loader:
        default_format:      json
        include_format:      false
```

This code fragment instructs the bundle to use default JSON as the default format
and not the include format. The `include_format` option when enabled adds a
special `{_format}` parameter to the routings to allow the requester to choose the
preferred output format (that is, JSON or XML).

At the end, add a new file to `config.yml` as follows:

```
imports:
    # ... other imports
    - { resource: fos/rest.yml }
```

NelmioApiDocBundle

The second bundle that we will configure is `NelmioApiDocBundle`. This bundle
really improves development in the areas of development and code testing. This
bundle handles automatic documentation generation just based on the annotated
documentation provided in the comments of your methods. Based on this, it allows
you to not only publish great documentation, but also, to test it by providing a
sandbox for method testing.

To configure this bundle, we will need to add a new config file in `app/config/
nelmio/api_doc.yml` and provide a basic configuration as follows:

```
nelmio_api_doc:
    name: TODO App
```

This will provide a title for the documentation page. This bundle, of course, contains
many more options, so it is again recommended to dig in to its documentation.

Again, we need to import our configuration in `config.yml` as follows:

```
imports:
    # .. previous bundles
    - { resource: fos/rest.yml }
    - { resource: nelmio/api_doc.yml }
```

To finalize the bundle configuration, we need to add it to the routing and we need to add security exception to allow the documentation to be viewed without logging in. Modify the `app/config/routing.yml` file, and add the following at the end:

```
NelmioApiDocBundle:
    resource: "@NelmioApiDocBundle/Resources/config/routing.yml"
    prefix:   /api/doc
```

This will add the `/api/doc` routing with an automatically generated documentation to our API. To access this without being logged in, we need to add security exception in our access control section. Add the following at the beginning of the section:

```
access_control:
    - { path: ^/api/doc$, role: IS_AUTHENTICATED_ANONYMOUSLY }
    # ...
```

FOSJSRoutingBundle

When developing the JavaScript calls, developers can often face a problem with dynamically changing routing. Sometimes during the refactoring, some methods change the URL. Usually, even switching to the development mode can slightly change the URL by prefixing it with `/app_dev.php/`. To avoid complex URL changes, it is recommended to install and configure this bundle. It will allow you to expose the selected routings to JavaScript, and then use JavaScript methods to generate the URLs.

This bundle does not require configuration, but it needs to be correctly placed (by executing the `assets:install` command) and it needs to be added to the `javascripts` section and the `routing` section. First, add the following to `app/config/routing.yml` at the end:

```
fos_js_routing:
    resource: "@FOSJsRoutingBundle/Resources/config/routing/routing.xml"
```

Next, issue the following command:

```
$ php app/console assets:install --symlink web/
```

Then, modify the app/Resources/views/base.html.twig file's javascripts block:

```twig
{% block javascripts %}
    <script src="https://ajax.googleapis.com/ajax/libs/jquery/2.1.3/
jquery.min.js"></script>
    <script src="{{ asset('bundles/fosjsrouting/js/router.js') }}"></
script>
    <script src="{{ path('fos_js_routing_js', { 'callback': 'fos.
Router.setData' }) }}"></script>

    {% javascripts
        'js/vendor/semantic-ui/semantic.min.js'
        'js/dev/app.js'
        output='/js/app.js'
    %}
        <script src="{{ asset_url }}"></script>
    {% endjavascripts %}
{% endblock %}
```

In the preceding code, we have added two new JavaScript calls. This needs to be added as early as possible, as it will expose the Routing object and the Routing.generate() method with the same parameters as Twig's path() function. However, note that FOSJSRoutingBundle only generates the routing specifically exposed to JS. We will handle this later when we add our API controller.

Refactoring the existing code

Now, it's time to modify our view template in views/tasks/list.html.twig. We need to refactor it a little. Firstly, we need to add a new column with actions, and secondly, we need to put our form in separate Twig files.

The changes in our action table are marked as follows:

```twig
<table class="ui blue table">
    <thead>
        <tr>
            <th>{{ 'todo_list.name'|trans }}</th>
            <th>{{ 'todo_list.notes'|trans }}</th>
            <th>{{ 'todo_list.tags'|trans }}</th>
            <th>{{ 'todo_list.due'|trans }}</th>
            <th>{{ 'todo_list.actions'|trans }}</th>
        </tr>
    </thead>
    <tbody>
        {% for task in tasks %}
```

```
<tr data-task-id="{{ task.id }}">
    <td>{{ task.name }}</td>
    <td>{{ task.notes }}</td>
    <td>
        {% for tag in task.tags %}
        <span class="ui tag label">{{ tag.name }}</span>
        {% endfor %}
    </td>
    <td>
        {{ task.dueDate is empty ? "" : task.
dueDate|date('Y-m-d') }}
    </td>
    <td>
        <a href="#" class="action" data-action="edit"><i
class="edit icon"></i></a>
        <a href="#" class="action" data-action="finish"><i
class="checkmark icon"></i></a>
        <a href="#" class="action" data-action="delete"><i
class="remove icon"></i></a>
    </td>
</tr>
```

This will add a new column, and provide some nice action icons for each task entered in the system. Also, we have provided some `data-` attributes for our JavaScript code. Now we need to refactor our form. Currently, it is handled within the same template file, but now we also need to use it for editing. Instead of duplicating the code, we will create a new file in `app/Resources/views/task/form.html.twig` with the following content:

```
{% form_theme form 'Form/theme.html.twig' %}

<p>{{ 'todo_list.new'|trans }}</p>
<div id="todo_form" style="width: 585px;">
    <form method="POST" action="{{ path('homepage', { id: app.request.
get('id') }) }}" class="ui form small" novalidate="novalidate">
        {{ form_widget(form) }}
    </form>
</div>
```

In our original `list.html.twig` file, we will use a new tag as follows:

```
{# previous part of the template #}
</table>

<div id="todo_form">
    {% include 'task/form.html.twig' %}
```

```
    </div>
{% endblock %}
```

By default, the `include` function will expose all the template variables to the imported template ones. In our case, the `form` variable will be available also within the `form.html.twig` template.

Finally, remove the `javascripts` block completely from `list.html.twig`. It will be properly added to the external JavaScript file.

Adding a new controller

Now we need to add the main API controller. Add a new `Controller` file named `TaskApiController.php`. This controller is presented as follows along with comments to the specific parts of the code:

```php
<?php

namespace AppBundle\Controller;

use AppBundle\Entity\Task;
use AppBundle\Form\Type\TaskType;
use FOS\RestBundle\Controller\FOSRestController;
use Symfony\Component\HttpFoundation\JsonResponse;
use Symfony\Component\HttpFoundation\Request;
use Nelmio\ApiDocBundle\Annotation\ApiDoc;
use Symfony\Component\HttpKernel\Exception\NotFoundHttpException;

class TaskApiController extends FOSRestController
{
```

Note that here we do not by default extend the controller, instead we use `FOSRestController`. Also, we need to import the `ApiDoc` annotation to provide support for `ApiDocBundle`. While this class is used only within annotation, it still needs to be imported here.

```php
    /**
     * @param $id
     * @return Task|null
     */
    protected function retrieveTask($id)
    {
        $em = $this->getDoctrine()->getManager();

        $task = $em->getRepository('AppBundle:Task')
```

```
            ->createQueryBuilder('t')
            ->where('t.id = :id')
            ->setParameter('id', $id)
            ->getQuery()
            ->getOneOrNullResult();

    if (null === $task) {
        throw new NotFoundHttpException();
    }

    return $task;
}
```

The preceding code is a simple helper method. Note this method's lack of security. In normal conditions, we would check whether the requester actually has permissions to load the object (is the owner of this). In real live projects, always remember to check the objects security. The helper will automatically throw a 404 exception when no task is found. In the production mode, this will result in a basic 404 page, and on the development mode, it will produce a stack trace with the information of how and when the exception was thrown:

```
    /**
     * Load new form and return HTML content
     *
     * @ApiDoc(
     *     parameters={
     *         { "name"="id", "dataType"="integer", "required"=true,
     * "description"="Task Database ID" }
     *     },
     *     statusCodes={
     *         200="Loaded new form content",
     *         404="did not found object",
     *         500="Unhandled Exception - something went very wrong"
     *     }
     * )
     */
    public function getTaskAction(Request $request, $id)
    {
        $task = $this->retrieveTask($id);

        $form = $this->createForm(new TaskType(), $task, ['em' =>
$this->getDoctrine()->getManager()]);
```

```
        return $this->render('task/form.html.twig', [
            'form' => $form->createView()
        ]);
    }
```

In this method, the real fun and magic begins. First of all, it contains a large structured comment. This comment will be used to generate documentation, describe parameters, and configure the sandbox mode.

The name of the getTaskAction method will be used by FOSRestBundle to automatically create the [GET] /[prefix]/tasks/{id} routing. The method renders the same part of the template that we are using in our list.html.twig template, only this time while processing, the URL of the form (within the form tag) will be changed to load the edited form object:

```
    /**
     * Updates Task Status as finished
     *
     * @ApiDoc(
     *     parameters={
     *         { "name"="id", "dataType"="integer", "required"=true,
     "description"="Task Database ID" }
     *     },
     *     statusCodes={
     *         200="Task finished correctly",
     *         404="did not found object",
     *         500="Unhandled Exception - something went very wrong"
     *     }
     * )
     */
    public function finishTaskAction(Request $request, $id)
    {
        $em = $this->getDoctrine()->getManager();

        $task = $this->retrieveTask($id);
        $task->setFinished(true);
        $em->persist($task);
        $em->flush();

        return new JsonResponse(['status' => 'ok']);
    }
```

The same method is implemented here. This method is responsible for finalizing a task. Note a few points as follows:

- We are loading and then updating the object through the entity manager. Always remember to persist the changed object and to flush the changes.

- We are returning the response in JSON format using one of the Symfony2 standard response classes. The class accepts array as an argument and will produce the JSON response along with all the required headers.

- The finishTaskAction method will result as a [PATCH] /[prefix]/ tasks/{$id}/finish routing. You can, of course, override this using special FOSRestBundle annotations:

```
/**
 * Delete given task from the database
 *
 * @ApiDoc(
 *      parameters={
 *          { "name"="id", "dataType"="integer",
"required"=true, "description"="Task Database ID" }
 *      },
 *      statusCodes={
 *          200="Task deleted",
 *          404="did not found object",
 *          500="Unhandled Exception - something went very
wrong"
 *      }
 * )
 */
public function deleteTaskAction(Request $request, $id)
{
    $em = $this->getDoctrine()->getManager();
    $task = $this->retrieveTask($id);

    $em->remove($task);
    $em->flush();

    return $this->handleView($this->view(['status' => 'ok'],
200));
    }
}
```

Finally, comes the delete action. Note how each comment in controller method is created, how description of method varies. This is important, because the real documentation will be created based on this.

The `deleteTask` will result in the creation of `[DELETE] /[prefix]/tasks/{id}`, so it will actually require a `HTTP DELETE` request to be executed. If you execute the delete action with any other request, it will be rejected with the **405 Method Not Allowed** status.

In this method we have deleted the entity. Note in this case that we also need to execute the flush command, otherwise the real `SQL DELETE` statement will not be executed.

Setting up routing and JavaScript

Now, after we have created this controller, we need to bind it to the routing. Open `app/config/routing.yml` and add the following to the end:

```
api:
    resource: "@AppBundle/Controller/TaskApiController.php"
    prefix:   /api
    type:     rest
    options:  { expose: true }
```

The first two lines look pretty standard, just like the one we created in app routing. The prefix line will add the prefix to all the routings created within this resource (so `prefix` in our previous examples will be replaced with `api`). Also, the REST type is meaningful. It is used by `FOSRestBundle` to trigger the REST bundle functionality, especially the routing generation, response content-negotiation handling, and so on.

Finally, `FOSJSRoutingBundle` uses the expose option to expose all the content to the JavaScript routing.

When you add everything, you should see the generated docs under the `/api/doc` URL as per the following screenshot:

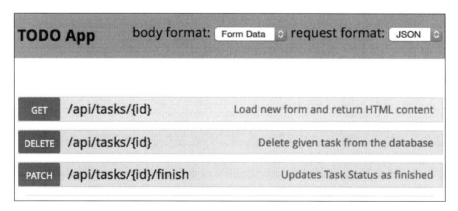

Play a little with this documentation. When you click on each of the titles, your documents will be presented. You can even issue some sample queries and review responses.

Now we need to add our JavaScript to the handle and bind everything. Add the following code to `web/js/dev/app.js`:

```
$(function() {
    $('.dropdown').dropdown();

    $('.action').click(function() {
        var self = $(this);
        var action = self.data('action');
        var taskId = self.parents('tr').data('task-id');

        if (action == 'edit') {
            $("#todo_form").load(Routing.generate('get_task', { id:
taskId }), function() {
                $('.dropdown').dropdown();
            });
        } else if (action == 'finish') {
            $.ajax({
                url: Routing.generate('finish_task', { id: taskId }),
                method: 'PATCH',
                success: function(data) {
                    if (data.status == 'ok') {
                        self.parents('tr').remove();
                    }
                }
            });
        } else if (action == 'delete') {
            $.ajax({
                url: Routing.generate('delete_task', { id: taskId }),
                method: 'DELETE',
                success: function(data) {
                    if (data.status == 'ok') {
                        self.parents('tr').remove();
                    }
                }
            });
        }

        return false;
    });
});
```

Note that in every AJAX call, we are using routes generated dynamically by
FOSJSRoutingBundle. If you want to check which routes are exposed, issue the
following command:

```
$ php app/console fos:js-routing:debug
```

You should see something similar to this:

```
[router]  Current routes

 Name          Method Scheme Host Path

 finish_task PATCH   ANY    ANY  /api/tasks/{id}/finish

 get_task    GET     ANY    ANY  /api/tasks/{id}

 delete_task DELETE  ANY    ANY  /api/tasks/{id}
```

This method will allow you to verify that everything is fine, and also, here you can
see the generated routing name. After modifying the app.js file, build its production
version with the following command:

```
$ php app/console assetic:dump --env=prod
```

You can now start testing your work.

Summary

In this chapter, we have extended our knowledge on how to handle doctrine models,
we have got some ideas on how to handle AJAX, and generally, how to write API
code and document it, and what kind of bundles can be used to automate and speed
up development.

In the next chapter, we will focus on some background tasks, writing and executing
cron tasks, and sending automated e-mails.

8
Command-line Operations

While developing a web application, we often have a requirement to process a large amount of data or to create some kind of repeatable automated job.

Symfony2 comes with a component, called the console component, to help us with such tasks. This component, just like Twig or Forms, can be installed as a standalone PHP library, and it is available in Symfony2 out of the box.

In fact, we have been using this component since the beginning—the Symfony2 `app/console` command is just a set of console component classes.

In this chapter, we will cover the following topics:

- Adding our own command to the Symfony2 console
- How to send e-mails with the swiftmailer component
- How to write custom logs

Creating the console command

To create the console command, we need to create a special class with the `Command` suffix. This suffix is required so that Symfony2 can find and automatically attach your class to the Symfony2 application console.

See the following example of the basic command:

```php
<?php

// File src/AppBundle/Command/HelloCommand.php
namespace AppBundle\Command;

use Symfony\Component\Console\Command\Command;
```

```
use Symfony\Component\Console\Input\InputInterface;
use Symfony\Component\Console\Output\OutputInterface;

class HelloCommand extends Command
{
    protected function configure()
    {
        $this
            ->setName('todo:hello')
            ->setDescription('this is simple, hello command')
        ;
    }

    protected function execute(
        InputInterface $input,
        OutputInterface $output
    )
    {
        $output->writeln('Hello world!');
    }
}
```

When you add this file and execute the app/console command, you would see that it has been attached to your console set under a new todo namespace. To work properly, each command class needs to have two methods added to it, as shown in the preceding example. In the configure method, we will define the name, description (visible on the console output), as well as any required or optional argument and option. We are putting the code to be executed in the execute method. This command accepts two variables, one to handle the input data and one to handle the output.

Now, let's try to extend this. The console component allows you to easily add options and arguments to your command. It also allows you to output the results using some basic formatting, changing colors, and so on. Modify the Hello class as follows:

```
protected function configure()
{
    $this
        ->setName('todo:hello')
        ->setDescription('this is simple, hello command')
        ->addArgument('name', null, 'What is your name?', 'World')
    ;
}
```

```
protected function execute(InputInterface $input, OutputInterface
$output)
{
    $name = $input->getArgument('name');
    $output->writeln(sprintf('<info>Hello %s!</info>', $name));
}
```

What we did is that we added a new optional argument with a default `World` value, and we reformatted the output.

To add the argument, we used the `addArgument` method. This method can take the following syntax:

```
addArgument($name, $mode = null, $description = '', $default = null)
```

In the preceding code:

- `name` is the argument name.
- `mode` is an `InputArgument::OPTIONAL` (default) or `InputArgument::REQUIRED` constant. The class exists within the `Symfony\Component\Console\Input` namespace.
- `description` is the argument description that is visible when you type `help`.
- `default` is the default value added when no value is provided.

Now, when you execute this command with the `help` option, you would see something similar to this:

```
$ php app/console todo:hello --help
Usage:
 todo:hello [name]

Arguments:
 name                   What is your name? (default: "World")

Options:
 --help (-h)            Display this help message
 --quiet (-q)           Do not output any message
 --verbose (-v|vv|vvv) Increase the verbosity of messages: 1 for normal
output, 2 for more verbose output and 3 for debug
 --version (-V)         Display this application version
 --ansi                 Force ANSI output
 --no-ansi              Disable ANSI output
 --no-interaction (-n) Do not ask any interactive question
 --shell (-s)           Launch the shell.
```

```
--process-isolation    Launch commands from shell as a separate process.
--env (-e)             The Environment name. (default: "dev")
--no-debug             Switches off debug mode.
```

Note that your added argument has a description that you entered, and it is marked as optional. Apart from your argument, you may notice that we have some standard Symfony2 options added, such as help, quiet, and so on. These options are always added, so you don't have to bother setting the options such as environment and debug. Also, you can use them to configure the debug or verbosity level as required. If there will be an error within your command, using options like verbose will automatically add a stack trace to help you track the error.

Now check the output of the command by typing the following:

```
$ php app/console todo:hello John
```

You may notice that the command output is presented in green color. The console component by default supports outputting with few styles:

- info: This is with green color text
- comment: This is with yellow color text
- question: This is with black text and a cyan background
- error: This is with a red background and white text

Try to replace and experiment with your console code to see the different outputs, that is, replace info with error in our example code:

```
$output->writeln(sprintf('<error>Hello %s!</error>', $name));
```

Apart from arguments, you can also add options. The difference between arguments and options is that arguments need to be passed in a specific order, while options can be passed in any order, as and when you define the name of the option when you use it.

Now let's do the real task for this chapter. To make the analysis easier, the code will be split into fragments as follows:

```php
<?php

// src/AppBundle/Command/SendCommand
namespace AppBundle\Command;

use Symfony\Bundle\FrameworkBundle\Command\ContainerAwareCommand;
use Symfony\Component\Console\Input\InputInterface;
use Symfony\Component\Console\Output\OutputInterface;
```

```
class SendCommand extends ContainerAwareCommand
{
    protected function configure()
    {
        $this
            ->setName('todo:send-reminder')
            ->setDescription('send email reminder');
    }
```

The preceding code will generate the required configuration for the console command. You may notice that the class is extended with a different base class called ContainerAwareCommand. This class is provided by Symfony2 and gives access to the Symfony2 dependency injection container, where you can access various services such as the mailer and entity manager:

```
    protected function execute(InputInterface $input, OutputInterface
$output)
    {
        $em = $this
            ->getContainer()
            ->get('doctrine.orm.entity_manager');

        $today = new \DateTime();

        $tasks = $em->getRepository('AppBundle:Task')
            ->createQueryBuilder('t')
            ->select('t.id, t.name, t.notes, u.email, u.username')
            ->innerJoin('t.user', 'u')
            ->where('t.due_date = :today')
            ->andWhere('t.finished = false')
            ->setParameter('today', $today->format('Y-m-d'))
            ->getQuery()
            ->getArrayResult()
        ;
        // ...
    }
}
```

In this code fragment, we are using the container method and getting our entity manager. Note that the class we are using is called differently now. Since we don't need to modify the result set, it is recommended not to hydrate into objects, but to rely on a simple array hydration, which is much quicker. Also, this allows us to select the data required by us and not the whole object.

We will stop for a moment with our code. Now, when we have got the results, we are ready to prepare the e-mail message and we can send our reminders. To do so, we need to use a mailer service. Symfony2 provides a default swiftmailer component to handle the job, but you can, of course, use your own.

Swiftmailer

As mentioned earlier, Symfony2 provides a default mailer component called swiftmailer. Its default configuration looks like this:

```
# app/config/config.yml
# ...
# Swiftmailer Configuration
swiftmailer:
    transport: "%mailer_transport%"
    host:      "%mailer_host%"
    username:  "%mailer_user%"
    password:  "%mailer_password%"
    spool:     { type: memory }
```

The parameters are taken from the `parameters.yml` file. By default, swiftmailer sends from a locally configured SMTP host, so check your configuration and adapt it as required.

There is one configuration tweak added by default to `config_dev.yml` (so working only in the development mode):

```
#swiftmailer:
#    delivery_address: me@example.com
```

When uncommented and configured, it will cause swiftmailer to send any e-mail to this specific address, while in the development mode. This is a very useful option, as it allows us to test any e-mail to be sent to any user without sending the real e-mail to them.

 This is only a basic list of options. The full list of options can be found in the Symfony2 reference documentation at `http://symfony.com/doc/current/reference/configuration/swiftmailer.html`.

Let's get back to our code. After we fetch our tasks, we need to send an e-mail for each of the tasks that are due today. To send an e-mail, we need to prepare a message as follows:

```
foreach ($tasks as $task) {
  $output->writeln('Sending email to: '. $task['email']);
```

```
$message = \Swift_Message::newInstance()
    ->setSubject('Task Reminder: '. $task['name'])
    ->setFrom('no-reply@mytodoapp.com')
    ->setTo($task['email'])
    ->setBody($this
        ->getContainer()
        ->get('templating')
        ->render('Email/reminder.html.twig',
            ['task' => $task]
        ), 'text/html'
    )
;
```

In the preceding fragment, we are setting up a basic message. What is worth noticing here is how we fetch the body. In our case, we are calling the templating service, and providing a Twig template (described later). We were using this service before within the controller. However, the controller class provides a `$this->render()` shortcut method; while in command you need to call the full service name.

When a method is prepared, we will send it as follows:

```
try {
    $mailer = $this
        ->getContainer()
        ->get('mailer')
        ->send($message);
} catch (\Exception $e) {
    $output->writeln('<error>'. $e->getMessage()
.'<error>');
    }
    }
    }
}
```

In case of error, an exception will be thrown and displayed in the console.

Now we need to add the promised template, as follows:

```
{# app/Resources/views/Email/reminder.html.twig #}
<html>
    <head>
        <style type="text/css">
            body { font-family: Helvetica, Arial, sans-serif; }
        </style>
    </head>
    <body>
```

```
<p>
    Hello {{ task.username }},</p>

<p>This is a gently reminder about your task due today:</p>

<p>
    <strong>Your task details:</strong>
</p>

<p>
    <strong>{{ task.name }}</strong><br />
    {{ task.notes }}
</p>
<p>
    Kind Regards,<br />
    Your To Do App
</p>
</body>
</html>
```

Note in the preceding code how we used arrays in Twig. In fact, there is no difference whether we use arrays or objects, we can access both of them in the same way. This is very convenient, as it allows the switching between objects and arrays with minimal effort when optimizing or refactoring code.

Finally, we can test our method, and see the e-mail in our mailbox. Remember to properly configure swiftmailer in `config.yml` and to enable the delivery address in the development mode.

Logging

To make our application more elegant while working in cron, we should implement logging to a file. Symfony2 supports some standard logs, through the so-called monolog component. To use this, we simply call for the logger service, and then we call the required method, either the `info`, `err`, `debug`, `notice` methods or the `warn` method, as in the following example:

```
$logger = $this->getContainer()->get('logger');
$logger->info('Info log message');
```

This log message will add to the default log (development or production) depending on the environment.

We need to change this a little bit, to allow the logs to be added to a separate file.

To do this, we need to define the channel and handler. When we create a channel, a separate logger service is created, and we can use it to log information here. Creating a simple channel is easy, as we just need to pass its name into the channel's array in the `config` file. After we add the channel, we need to add the handler, so that monolog would know what to do with the information logged in it.

Add the following code at the bottom of `config.yml`:

```
monolog:
    channels: ['mail']
    handlers:
        mail:
            # log all messages (since debug is the lowest level)
            level:    debug
            type:     stream
            path:     "%kernel.logs_dir%/mail.log"
            channels: [mail]
```

This code will add a single channel and handler to the file. Note the level of messages added. The debug level will guarantee that you will see every message. Next, we will define the type of the message, path where to store, and what channels are handled in it.

Now, when we have configured our custom logger, we can add them to our file to log the required information. To call the logger for our custom channel, we simply call a service with the name, `monolog.logger.<channel>`. In our case, add the following:

```
// previously added code
$em = $this
    ->getContainer()
    ->get('doctrine.orm.entity_manager');

// adding logger service
$logger = $this
    ->getContainer()
    ->get('monolog.logger.mail');
```

Now we can add our logging information to the following:

```
foreach ($tasks as $task) { // previous code
    $output->writeln('Sending email to: '. $task['email']);
    // adding logger
    $logger->info('Sending email to: ' . $task['email']. 'with
reminder about task: '. $task['id']);
    // ...
```

Add the following lines, too:

```
} catch (\Exception $e) {
    $output->writeln('<error>'. $e->getMessage() .'<error>');
    $logger->error($e->getMessage());
}
```

Now, when the command sends an e-mail, it will be logged in a separate logger file.

 If you want to test error logging, please make sure the spool: line in config.yml is commented out, otherwise swiftmailer will not return issues with e-mail sending directly after you call the send method.

Summary

In this chapter, we dug into the console system, we learned how to send e-mails, and we created our own logger. These are basic tasks, usually needed when creating background or cron jobs.

In the next chapter, we will focus on the Symfony2 profiler and debugger to make debugging more efficient.

9
Symfony2 Profiler and Debugger

Easy debugging and profiling of your applications is often one of the most crucial things that is required when developing an application, giving you the ability to easily profile and debug various variables and events.

In this chapter, we will do the following:

- Learn about the Web Debug Toolbar
- Examine the possibilities of Symfony2 profiler
- Add a new section to Symfony2 profiler
- Add our own stopwatch

The Web Debug Toolbar

Symfony2 comes with one built-in tool capable of making our life much easier. This tool is called the Web Debug Toolbar. The Web Debug Toolbar is the element sitting at the bottom of the page, and it gives you access to the full profiler page.

When you launch the to-do application, you should see a little Symfony2 icon on the right-bottom corner of the screen. Click on this icon. After you do this, you should see something similar to the following screenshot (without the first three sections):

The first section visible on this screen describes the controller used to display this page, action, and routing name. Also, it shows the status code returned by the controller. If you wish to have more detailed information, hover on the element (do not click on it yet).

The next section describes the AJAX requests passed to the controller. In the current state, there are no AJAX requests. We will try to create one later on.

The third visible section is a timer, that is, the total time to process and display the page.

The next parameter describes the memory usage, and when you hover over it, this will also give you the information about the total memory limit.

The fifth section displays information about the form object. Since the login page doesn't use form type and form object, here it displays **0** detected forms. We will discuss this part later on, when we proceed to our list page.

The sixth section displays information about the logged in user. It is worth to notice that even if you are an anonymous user, you are still authenticated, but as an anonymous user.

The last visible section on this bar is the database query counter. As the login page doesn't use the database unless the form is submitted, this also shows a zero value.

The three sections that are not visible on the screen will simply output the following:

- Symfony2 version (with a link to documentation)
- PHP version (with a link to `phpinfo`)
- Application runtime configuration (that is, environment, application name, and profiler token)

The Symfony2 profiler

The profiler information is collected and stored within the cache directory and stored in simple serialized data files. You can access them by the token generated, and they will persist as long as the file exists in the cache folder.

The Web Debug Toolbar is displayed only in the development mode. If you run your configuration in the production mode, it will not be displayed, and it is not recommended to change this setting.

After you log in, you should notice changes in the form section and in the database section. Click on the form section to see something similar to this:

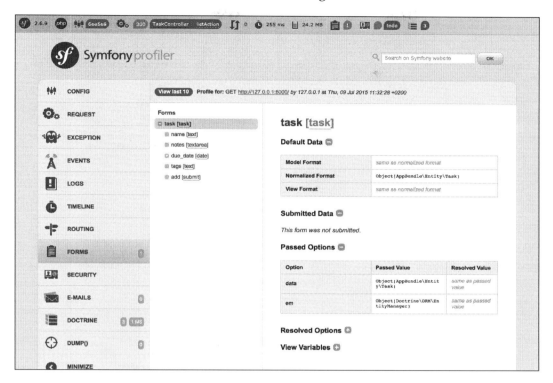

This is one of the most useful screens while debugging to check what went wrong with the form object. In the middle column, you have exposed all the form widgets that have been applied to. In the right column, you have information about the passed objects, model, and submitted data.

This section is most useful while checking why the form did not validate properly. So let's try to generate some errors to see what is happening. Since Symfony2 is generating HTML5 compatible required attributes, if you have a browser with HTML5 support, prior to testing this, you should remove the HTML5 validation. Change the highlighted line in the following form:

```
{# file: app/Resources/views/task/form.html.twig #}
{% form_theme form 'Form/theme.html.twig' %}

<p>{{ 'todo_list.new'|trans }}</p>
<div id="todo_form" style="width: 585px;">
```

```
        <form method="POST" action="{{ path('homepage', { id: app.request.
    get('id') }) }}" class="ui form small" novalidate="novalidate">
            {{ form_widget(form) }}
        </form>
    </div>
```

Now let's try to submit the form without filling any data. The form will display an error near the name field, and the profiler will flag the form error with red color on the form counter. Click on the form profile section again, and click on the flagged **name** section to see the following:

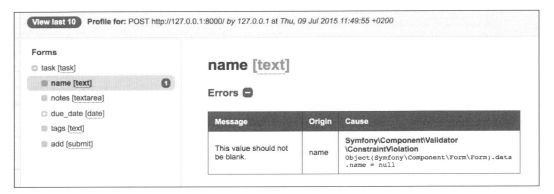

As you can see, you can determine which field flagged the error, which validator is responsible for this, and what the message was. This view is very helpful in situations with more complicated forms and many validation groups.

Another very valuable section is the doctrine section. It will flag all the queries that you have executed, the time of execution, and potentially, it will warn you about long-running queries or invalid entities.

The profiler sections

Along with the database and form queries, the default profiler menu also contains the following:

- **Config**: This section displays the current project server, configuration, and app bundles information.

- **Request**: This section displays information about the request objects—GET and POST, cookies, and other valuable information.

- **Exception**: This returns information about uncaught exceptions.

- **Events**: This displays information about active, registered event listeners and which of them has been called.

- **Logs**: This displays the monolog logs. You can filter the logs by priority. You would notice a few warning messages about the missing translations.

- **Timeline**: This section will give you profiler information about the total time required for initialization and the execution time. This is your basic view when you are looking for a way to optimize your code.

- **Routing**: This section will show you the details about your current matched routing.

- **Security**: This section displays the user role and assigned roles.

- **E-mails**: This section displays information about the e-mails sent.

- **Dump**: This section allows you to catch dumped variables, and display their content here.

There is quite a lot of data that we can analyze, and we have a lot of information out of the box.

VarDumper

The `dump` section is controlled by the newly introduced component called VarDumper. Note that, by default, it is available only in the development mode, so if you execute it in production, it will end up with error 500 (internal server), because the function will not be loaded.

To show how VarDumper works, add the following change to your controller:

```
// src/AppBundle/Controller/TaskController.php
$tasks = $em->getRepository('AppBundle:Task')
    ->createQueryBuilder('t')
    ->where('t.finished = :finished')
    ->andWhere('t.user = :user')
    ->orderBy('t.due_date', 'ASC')
    ->setParameter('finished', false)
    ->setParameter('user', $this->getUser())
    ->getQuery()
    ->getResult();

// add variable dump
dump(['hello' => 'world!']);
dump($request);
dump($tasks);
```

Now, refresh your homepage view.

You would notice the new section in the Web Debug Toolbar. When you click on it, you will see the dumped variable, and you will be able to review the variable content interactively and in a more elegant way than the standard `var_dump` or `print_r` methods.

The AJAX requests

It is, also, possible to debug the AJAX requests using the profiler. You can try to mark one of your tasks as finished, and observe the Web Debug Toolbar AJAX component.

When the AJAX request is detected, a separate profile ID is provided within it, so you can review all the data for that request (POST data, dumped variables, and so on).

Data collectors

Now, it's time to discover a way to create your own profile section. Adding this might be useful if you are developing your own bundle and you want to give other developers an easy way to debug your code. To add the profile section, you need to create a new data collector. Let's assume that we want to track information about how many tasks and tags we have in the database.

Add the following code:

```php
<?php

// src/AppBundle/Collector/TaskDataCollector
namespace AppBundle\Collector;

use Doctrine\ORM\EntityManager;
use Symfony\Component\HttpFoundation\Request;
use Symfony\Component\HttpFoundation\Response;
use Symfony\Component\HttpKernel\DataCollector\DataCollector;

class TaskDataCollector extends DataCollector
{
    /**
     * @var EntityManager
     */
    protected $em;

    public function __construct(EntityManager $em)
    {
        $this->em = $em;
    }
```

In the constructor, we will inject entity manager through our service
container configuration:

```
    public function collect(Request $request, Response $response, \
Exception $exception = null)
    {
        $em = $this->em;

        $tasks = $em->getRepository('AppBundle:Task')
            ->createQueryBuilder('t')
            ->select('count(t.id)')
            ->getQuery()
            ->getSingleScalarResult();

        $tags = $em->getRepository('AppBundle:Tag')
            ->createQueryBuilder('t')
            ->select('count(t.id)')
            ->getQuery()
            ->getSingleScalarResult();

        $this->data = array(
            'tasks' => $tasks,
            'tags' => $tags
        );
    }
```

The collector method is used to collect and serialize data. When extending the
`DataCollector` object, it will automatically serialize the data property, so make
sure that all the data stored within it can be serialized:

```
    public function getTasks()
    {
        return $this->data['tasks'];
    }

    public function getTags()
    {
        return $this->data['tags'];
    }

    public function getName()
    {
        return 'tasks';
    }
}
```

The getters, setters, and name method are required by `DataCollectorInterface`.

Now, we need to prepare a template to display the data. Add the following code:

```twig
{# app/Resources/views/collectors/tasks.html.twig #}
{% extends 'WebProfilerBundle:Profiler:layout.html.twig' %}

{% block toolbar %}
    {% set icon %}
        <span>
            <span class="sf-toolbar-status">{{ collector.tasks }}</span>
            <span class="sf-toolbar-status sf-toolbar-info-piece-additional">tasks</span>
        </span>
    {% endset %}

    {% set text %}
        <div class="sf-toolbar-info-piece">
            <b>No of tasks</b>
            <span>{{ collector.tasks }} tasks</span>
        </div>
        <div class="sf-toolbar-info-piece">
            <b>No of tags</b>
            <span>{{ collector.tags }} tags</span>
        </div>
    {% endset %}

    {# Set the "link" value to false if you do not have a big "panel"
       section that you want to direct the user to. #}
    {% include '@WebProfiler/Profiler/toolbar_item.html.twig' with {
'link': false } %}
{% endblock %}
```

In the preceding template, we are defining the toolbar data, and the data is displayed when you hover over the taskbar. As creating a full page is very similar to the previous example and this is not within the scope of this book, we are marking the link parameter as false on the profiler page.

Note that in the template, you have access to the collector object, but only to properly unserialized variables.

Finally, we can bind our data together with a service configuration. Replace the data in `app/config/services.yml` with the following:

```
services:
    data_collector.tasks:
        class: AppBundle\Collector\TaskDataCollector
        arguments: ['@doctrine.orm.entity_manager']
        tags:
            - { name: data_collector, template: 'collectors/tasks.
html.twig', id: 'tasks' }
```

Note that in the ID, you need to use the same text as it was used in the `getName` method of `DataCollector`.

Now, when you refresh your application, you should see your new collector in action, that is, passing you the information about the number of tasks and tags in the database.

The stopwatch component

Since Symfony 2.2, the stopwatch component has been included in the standard Symfony. It allows you to measure time used in your various code fragments. You can add your own entries to the `timeline` section of the profile.

Amend the controller code as follows:

```
// src/AppBundle/Controller/TaskController
$watch = $this->get('debug.stopwatch');
$watch->start('Fetching Tasks');

$tasks = $em->getRepository('AppBundle:Task')
    ->createQueryBuilder('t')
    ->where('t.finished = :finished')
    ->andWhere('t.user = :user')
    ->orderBy('t.due_date', 'ASC')
    ->setParameter('finished', false)
    ->setParameter('user', $this->getUser())
    ->getQuery()
    ->getResult();

$watch->stop('Fetching Tasks');
```

Now, when you refresh and go to your profiler timeline section, you will see the additional fragment with the description of how much time it took to fetch and hydrate the tasks' objects.

Summary

In this chapter, we have learned how to efficiently debug and profile our web application. We have done a review of the profiler and web debug toolbar, and we added a custom data collector and stopwatch.

In the next chapter, we will focus on optimizations, setting up a project for production, and we will review a few strategies of how to deploy our project.

10
Preparing an Application for Production

When an app is ready, we need to prepare it for the production environment. The production environment usually has different settings and requirements. Preparing the Symfony2 application doesn't require much work, but there are steps that should be done and can be easily forgotten.

In this chapter, we will discuss the following topics:

- The steps to prepare an application for production
- Possible strategies for deployment
- Custom optimizations for error pages

Preparing an application

There are a few steps that you should consider while preparing your application for production. It usually involves the following steps:

1. Checking the code against debug variables or functions.
2. Customizing error pages.
3. Verifying the production server requirements.
4. Verifying the application against known framework security issues.
5. Updating the basic assets and metadata.

Let's discuss the preceding points.

Checking the code against debug code

Often, when you create your app, you are adding various debug codes to help you with debugging. Before deploying your work, it is important to verify how Symfony2 will behave in the production mode. Let's run our application and verify this. To run a built-in server in the production mode, execute the following:

```
$ php app/console server:run --env=prod
```

Now, when you run your app in the browser, you will notice that it doesn't have a web developer toolbar anymore, although the login page looks normal as usual. Let's try to log in. After you type your login ID, you will probably see an error 500 page. This is because in the previous chapter, we left the debug function within our controller.

Before we remove this, look into the production logs stored at app/logs/prod. log. By default, the Symfony2 logs in the developer environment contains a lot of information, to which you have access through the web debug toolbar and profiler (as discussed in *Chapter 9, Symfony2 Profiler and Debugger*). The production logs contain much less information; by default, they are used only when the application crashes. In most circumstances, this will be your primary source to learn what went wrong. When you open your log file, two important lines you will probably see are the following:

- php.EMERGENCY: Fatal Error: Call to undefined function AppBundle\Controller\dump() ...

- request.CRITICAL: Uncaught PHP Exception Symfony\Component\ Debug\Exception\UndefinedFunctionException: "Attempted to call function "dump" from namespace "AppBundle\Controller"." at ...

Along with the preceding lines, you will get the timestamp and location of the file where the error occurred. Let's go to this location, and we will see that our controller still has the dump() method, which is not available in the production mode.

We can either remove this (if we feel it will not be required), or we can make sure that we run it only in the development mode. Let's try the last option by modifying the controller and surrounding our dump functions with the environment condition, as follows:

```
// src/AppBundle/TaskController.php
if ($this->get('kernel')->getEnvironment() == 'dev') {
    dump(['hello' => 'world']);
    dump($request);
    dump($tasks);
}
```

Now everything should work as expected.

 The stopwatch service used to measure and profile time on the timeline section of the profiler, `debug.stopwatch` discussed in *Chapter 9, Symfony2 Profiler and Debugger*, is always available, so this does not require any detection or code fixing.

Customizing error pages

As we've seen in the production mode, there is an ugly basic version of the error 500 page. It should be probably replaced. Symfony2 supports three different kinds of error pages, as follows:

- **404 - Page Not Found**: This is displayed when no route has been found for the given address
- **403 - Access Denied**: This is displayed when a visitor does not have access to the page
- **500**: This is displayed for all the other errors, including the 500 code

To override the look and feel, we simply need to add files in the designated location to override the default ones.

Add the following new file:

```
{# app/Resources/TwigBundle/views/Exception/error404.html.twig #}
{% extends 'base.html.twig' %}

{% block body %}
    <h1>Page not found</h1>
    <p>Page you requested could not be found. Please try again.</p>
{% endblock %}
```

This will add a custom look to the 404 page. It will not work properly, because when we display the 404 page, we may not have access to our `app.user` object (it depends on firewall configuration and URL queried).

To avoid these issues, we also need to modify our `base.html.twig` as follows:

```
{# app/Resources/views/body.html.twig #}
<body>
  {% if app.user %}
  <div class="ui menu">
      <div class="item right">
```

```
        {% if is_granted('ROLE_USER') %}
            {{ 'top_menu.logged_in'|trans({ '%username%': app.user.
username }|raw }} | <a href="{{ path('fos_user_security_logout')
}}">{{ 'top_menu.logout'|trans }}</a>
        {% else %}
            <a href="{{ path('fos_user_registration_register')
}}">{{ 'top_menu.register'|trans }}</a>
        {% endif %}
    </div>
  </div>
  {% endif %}
```

This will ensure that we do not run into trouble. The last thing we need to do when we are working with production is to clear the cache. We can do this either by removing the `app/cache/*` content (but leaving the cache directory itself) or by typing in the console as follows:

```
$ app/console cache:clear --env=prod
```

After we do this, when we type some random URL, which does not match our routing, we should see a nice 404 page.

 You can look into the `vendors/symfony/symfony/src/Symfony/Bundle/TwigBundle/Resources/views/Exception` directory to see how the source file looks like, and how you can override others. Also, note that you can override a file not just for HTML, but also for JSON, JS, CSS, XML, and other formats.

Apart from modifying the look and feel of the error pages, we can also override the default exception controllers or PHP error handlers. The last option is very handy if we want to provide an automatic way for notifications about new errors that show up.

Symfony2 does provide bundles to integrate such custom error handlers (such as Errbit), and provides an extensive information about stack trace, the person who triggered the error, and sometimes the data that caused a problem. In most cases, having such system integration allows us to avoid the headache of interviewing an angry client.

Verifying the production server requirements

We have a handy tool to verify the production server requirements. We can check the requirements in both the command line (if we have access) or by accessing a special page directly on the server side.

As various systems may have a different php.ini file for the web server and a different php.ini for the command-line operations, it is recommended to check both to avoid any issues.

To execute the config check on the web server, you can simply upload the basic Symfony2 project, edit web/config.php by adding your IP address to the access rules, and type http://<yourserverdomain>/config.php. You should see something similar to this:

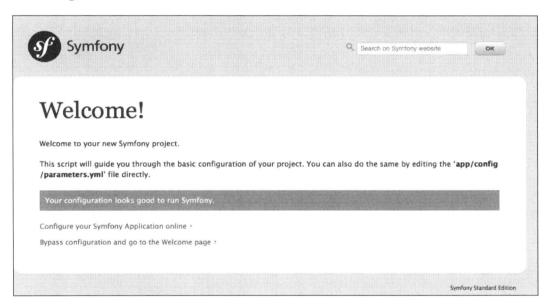

If you plan to run the console commands, you should also run the config checker from the command line, by typing the following:

```
$ php app/check.php
```

Verify that everything is fine. The requirements may vary from version to version, and the check script will let you know if any of the requirements fail and how important is for Symfony2 to have this.

Security check

Symfony2 does have a tool to verify against known security issues. If any of them are discovered, usually an upgrade will be recommended. To verify your app against known issues, type the following:

```
$ php app/console security:check
```

The expected result should look similar to the following:

```
Security Check Report
~~~~~~~~~~~~~~~~~~~~~~~

Checked file: /.../composer.lock

  [OK]
  0 packages have known vulnerabilities
```

It is good to show an example of this script when it shows an issue. The following code is executed against an older Symfony2 version with known security issues:

```
Checked file: /.../composer.lock

  [CRITICAL]
  1 packages have known vulnerabilities


symfony/symfony (v2.3.25)
-------------------------

 * CVE-2015-2309: Unsafe methods in the Request class
   http://symfony.com/blog/cve-2015-2309-unsafe-methods-in-the-request-
class

 * CVE-2015-4050: CVE-2015-4050: ESI unauthorized access
   http://symfony.com/blog/cve-2015-4050-esi-unauthorized-access

 * CVE-2015-2308: Esi Code Injection
   http://symfony.com/blog/cve-2015-2308-esi-code-injection
```

In such cases, it is usually best to follow the security advisories links and check what needs to be done to fix the issue. Usually, an update of the package quickly follows the advisory, so the best solution will be to update the package version through the composer.

Updating the basic assets and metadata

Symfony2 comes with a default favicon and Apple touch icon. It is good to replace these default icons, but it's often forgotten. Also, depending on your requirements, ensure that the meta tags are set correctly within the template.

Changing the web root directory

Sometimes, it is required to change the web root directory within a project. Usually, this situation happens when we need to deploy our application on a hosting environment, and the admin does not allow us to change the default directory structure.

With Symfony2, it is easy to change the web root directory (by default, it's a web directory). You can easily rename this to public or public_html, and this will also work without any issues. A more difficult case will be if you want to have Symfony2 in your project's root directory and not in the web directory. In this case, you need to move all the directories and files from the web directory to your desired location, edit the app.php file within it, and modify the path to your loader and kernel. This is shown in the following:

```php
<?php

use Symfony\Component\ClassLoader\ApcClassLoader;
use Symfony\Component\HttpFoundation\Request;

// modify this line as needed:
$loader = require_once __DIR__.'/../app/bootstrap.php.cache';

// Enable APC for autoloading to improve performance.
// You should change the ApcClassLoader first argument to a unique prefix
// in order to prevent cache key conflicts with other applications
// also using APC.
/*
$apcLoader = new ApcClassLoader(sha1(__FILE__), $loader);
$loader->unregister();
$apcLoader->register(true);
*/

// modify this line as needed:
require_once __DIR__.'/../app/AppKernel.php';
```

This is all that is required to change the web root directory.

Deployment strategies

When working with applications, there are often various limitations or preferences about how to handle application deployments. The most common ones are as follows:

- Copying the files through FTP (most difficult to proceed)
- Deploying through rsync
- Continuous Integration Deployment
- Deployment tools

FTP

The most unreliable and error-prone method is, of course, the FTP deployment. Not only does it take a long time, but it also does not easily allow to automate the process, and usually, does not allow to easily rollback the changes.

Before the deployment, it is good to clear the cache and empty the log folders to avoid transferring the files that are not project related. Also, ensure that you are not overwriting the `parameters.yml` file when redeploying the code.

All the post-deployment stuff, such as database migrations or assets management, needs to be either done on the developer machine and transferred (assets) or done manually. Multiple server deployment is very time consuming and involves the risk of having two different versions for a long time.

The rsync deployment

The rsync deployment is a more advanced solution, available if you have an SSH access to your deployment server but do not have a need for more advanced tools. The rsync deployment does have an advantage over FTP, as it allows us to deploy files quickly and easily and to ignore files during deployment.

There are some bundles that allow us to make this task easier. Usually, these bundles integrate rsync with `config.yml`, and allow us to define the post-deployment tasks. The disadvantage, just like with the previous systems, is that there is no way to rollback the changes, so before *rsyncing* you should create a backup.

Continuous integrations

The more advanced option, when it comes to deploy larger projects, is to have a **Continuous Integration (CI)** server. Symfony2 does not offer any help with this, but there are tons of guides to follow.

In this scenario, there is a well-known way to do this as follows:

1. Create a build script.
2. Integrate the CI system with our version control system.
3. Execute the build on the target server (either automatically or manually).

The CI systems, however, are more suitable for deploying code for automated unit testing, rather than for production servers. However, it is possible to also find them on this kind of task. While the process is automatic, it still does not have any way to rollback the changes easily after they are deployed.

Also, there is a lot of work involved in providing a way to share common files between the various builds (that is, files uploaded by users).

Deployment tools

As the name suggests, the deployment tools are designed to provide deployment. Some of the tools support Symfony2 directly, and they provide the following path:

1. Download a fresh copy of the code from Git.
2. Install the dependencies through the composer.
3. Configure the assets and permissions.
4. Configure the common paths.
5. Execute the additional tasks (that is, a Grunt or Gulp installation and execution).
6. Automatically apply the database migration patches.

The most popular tools known, when this book was written, are as follows:

- Capifony (based on Capistrano v2)
- Magellanes (a Capistrano-like tool, written in PHP)
- Fabric (a Python-based library)
- Deployer (new PHP deployment tool, with a built-in Symfony2 recipe similar to Capifony)

You can also write your own build script, but this is an option only when you have a very large and customized project.

To explain how deployment script works, most deployment tools create a directory structure similar to this:

```
current -> releases/20150603181758
releases
    20150602171330
    20150603162531
    20150603174511
    20150603181758
shared
    app
    web
```

The shared directory usually contains common files shared among all the releases through the symlink system. The versioning allows us to easily rollback to the previous version (this also includes database migrations, as doctrine migrations described in this book have the ability to rollback the changes). Deployments scripts usually follow the same pattern as follows:

- Connect to a target server
- Create a new version of the application
- Download the latest code (usually, the best approach is to deploy by connecting directly through Git, but it is possible to send code from the machine, which requested the deployment)
- Copy the code to the new version folder
- Create symlink to the so-called shared files
- Download and execute the composer script
- Execute the required commands, such as cache clear, assets publishing, and so on

If all the preceding steps are executed without any error, the deployment script will switch the application to the new version, by "symlinking" the current folder to the new version. If not, the deployment script will return an error, and the application will keep working on the old version without any issues.

Platform as a Service deployment

The official Symfony2 documentation and cookbook also provide some information about how to deploy a Symfony2 project on various PaaS providers, such as Azure and Heroku.

Summary

In this chapter, we have seen a few useful tips to polish our application and prepare it for deployment. Depending on the various requirements, your needs may differ.

This is the last chapter of the book. We have created a simple working application, learned how to debug it, how to prepare it for production, and deploy it.

This concludes a whole life cycle of the application, and hopefully, this book has shown to you how Symfony2 can make these tasks easier for you.

Index

S

SecurityBundleConfiguration section
  reference link 62
security handling 61, 62
Semantic UI
  URL 34
stopwatch component 119
stopwatch service 123
swiftmailer 106-108
Symfony
  history 2
  installing 3
  installing, through installer 4
  reasons, for selecting 1, 2
  URL 4
Symfony2
  built-in types 49
  constraints 51
  URL, for documentation 106
Symfony2 profiler
  about 112-114
  AJAX requests, debugging 116
  profiler sections 114, 115
  VarDumper 115, 116
Symfony console 12
Symfony directory structure
  about 5
  app 5
  bin 5
  src 5
  vendor 6
  web 6

T

task list
  creating 37-43
translation keys
  using 80-85
translations
  about 75
  file formats 77-79
  pluralization 79
  using, in controller 76, 77
  variables 79

translation strategy 80
Twig
  about 31
  concepts 31, 32
  URL 32
Twig templating engine
  about 31
  assets management 32

U

user manager bundle
  installing 63-71
users
  registering 71, 72

V

Vagrant
  URL 3
VarDumper
  working 115, 116
variables, translations 79
Views layer 20, 22

W

web debug toolbar 111, 112

Thank you for buying
Symfony2 Essentials

About Packt Publishing

Packt, pronounced 'packed', published its first book, *Mastering phpMyAdmin for Effective MySQL Management*, in April 2004, and subsequently continued to specialize in publishing highly focused books on specific technologies and solutions.

Our books and publications share the experiences of your fellow IT professionals in adapting and customizing today's systems, applications, and frameworks. Our solution-based books give you the knowledge and power to customize the software and technologies you're using to get the job done. Packt books are more specific and less general than the IT books you have seen in the past. Our unique business model allows us to bring you more focused information, giving you more of what you need to know, and less of what you don't.

Packt is a modern yet unique publishing company that focuses on producing quality, cutting-edge books for communities of developers, administrators, and newbies alike. For more information, please visit our website at www.packtpub.com.

About Packt Open Source

In 2010, Packt launched two new brands, Packt Open Source and Packt Enterprise, in order to continue its focus on specialization. This book is part of the Packt Open Source brand, home to books published on software built around open source licenses, and offering information to anybody from advanced developers to budding web designers. The Open Source brand also runs Packt's Open Source Royalty Scheme, by which Packt gives a royalty to each open source project about whose software a book is sold.

Writing for Packt

We welcome all inquiries from people who are interested in authoring. Book proposals should be sent to author@packtpub.com. If your book idea is still at an early stage and you would like to discuss it first before writing a formal book proposal, then please contact us; one of our commissioning editors will get in touch with you.

We're not just looking for published authors; if you have strong technical skills but no writing experience, our experienced editors can help you develop a writing career, or simply get some additional reward for your expertise.

Ext JS Essentials

ISBN: 978-1-78439-662-6   Paperback: 216 pages

Get up and running with building interactive and web applications using Sencha's Ext JS 5

1. Learn the Ext JS framework for developing rich web applications.

2. Understand how the framework works under the hood.

3. Explore the main tools and widgets of the framework for use in your own applications.

Extending Symfony2 Web Application Framework

ISBN: 978-1-78328-719-2   Paperback: 140 pages

Optimize, audit, and customize web applications with Symfony

1. Extend the main elements of Symfony 2.

2. Learn about the internal Symfony 2 framework.

3. Customize developed web applications with Symfony 2.

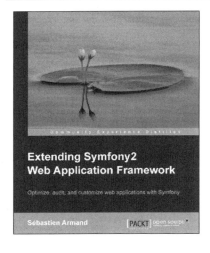

Please check **www.PacktPub.com** for information on our titles

[PACKT] open source ✿
PUBLISHING
community experience distilled

Laravel 5 Essentials

ISBN: 978-1-78528-301-7 Paperback: 144 pages

Explore the fundamentals of Laravel, one of the most expressive and robust PHP frameworks available

1. Create a dynamic web application that can read and write data to a database.

2. Improve your PHP skills and develop a new outlook on solving programming issues.

3. A step-by-step guide that covers the different steps involved in creating a complete Laravel application in an easy-to-understand manner.

Symfony 1.3

web application development

ISBN: 978-1-84719-456-5 Paperback: 228 pages

Design, develop, and deploy feature-rich, high-performance PHP web applications using the Symfony framework

1. Create powerful web applications by leveraging the power of this Model-View-Controller-based framework.

2. Covers all the new features of version 1.3 – many exciting plug-ins for you.

3. Learn by doing without getting into too much theoretical detail – create a "real-life" milkshake store application.

Please check **www.PacktPub.com** for information on our titles

7624082R00093

Printed in Germany
by Amazon Distribution
GmbH, Leipzig